VALUE FOR MONEY?

IMPACT OF SMALL ENTERPRISE DEVELOPMENT

Malcolm Harper
Gerry Finnegan

Prepared for the International Labour Office, South Asia
Multidisciplinary Advisory Team, New Delhi, and the
Entrepreneurship and Management Development Branch,
Geneva

INTERMEDIATE TECHNOLOGY PUBLICATIONS 1998

Practical Action Publishing Ltd
25 Albert Street, Rugby, CV21 2SD, Warwickshire, UK
www.practicalactionpublishing.com

© International Labour Organization, 1998

First published 1998\Digitised 2008

ISBN 13 Paperback: 9781853394362
ISBN Library Ebook: 9781780441009
Book DOI: http://dx.doi.org/10.3362/9781780441009

Since 1974, Practical Action Publishing has published and disseminated books and information in support of international development work throughout the world. Practical Action Publishing is a trading name of Practical Action Publishing Ltd (Company Reg. No. 1159018), the wholly owned publishing company of Practical Action. Practical Action Publishing trades only in support of its parent charity objectives and any profits are covenanted back to Practical Action (Charity Reg. No. 247257, Group VAT Registration No. 880 9924 76).

Foreword

The provocative question raised by the authors in the title of their book reflects a concern which has surfaced with increasing frequency, not only among donors, but also among serious practitioners involved in small enterprise promotion activities, to demonstrate that the benefits resulting from the activities in which they are engaged stand in a reasonable relationship to the costs involved.

While most would not question the need for more rigorous evaluation of small enterprise development projects and programmes, in practice, there have been relatively few who have attempted, let alone succeeded, in accurately quantifying benefits and costs of specific programmes. The reasons for this are many: projects often have multiple objectives, some of which are of a qualitative nature; other external influences affecting the target group and their businesses can be difficult or impossible to isolate; data are often hard to obtain; sustainability of benefits, in most cases a key concern, is often difficult to quantify and predict; it is not always clear what costs should be included. This makes it difficult to answer the question of whether a small enterprise development project really represents value for money.

Still, as is clearly demonstrated by the authors, a great deal has already been learnt in recent years with regard to what can be done to better answer the provocative question which they pose. One lesson is that evaluation should be taken into account at all stages of project design, planning, implementation and monitoring, and treated as an important part of the regular project management routines. While outsiders do have a role to play in more formal evaluations, those directly responsible for project implementation and, particularly, their small business clients, are best placed to carry out such evaluations. For the latter, this should include market-based feedback whereby clients indicate their perception of quality and relevance through a willingness to pay for at least part of the cost of the service provided.

There is little doubt that the systematic application of the guiding principles identified by the authors will substantially increase our understanding of the cost-effectiveness of projects as well as lay the foundation for improved project design and management. It is our experience, from a large number of ILO projects, that careful attention to evaluation and impact assessment, where it has been successfully undertaken, provides the raw data which is necessary to identify detailed lessons learnt from a project. This book contributes significantly to this important process.

M. Henriques
Chief
Entrepreneurship and Management Development Branch
International Labour Organization
Geneva

Contents

Preface

The International Labour Organization has been supporting small enterprise development programmes for almost 30 years. As the formal sector in many countries can offer only limited new employment opportunities, governments and their partners in development (such as ILO) are increasingly looking to the informal and small-scale sectors to generate new and sustainable employment opportunities. Therefore, it is particularly pertinent that this book addresses the issue of effectiveness and impact of small enterprise development programmes. By improving the effectiveness and impact of such programmes, governments and donors alike can be more assured that they are obtaining better "value for money" from their investment in SED support activities. In turn, target beneficiaries will derive more direct benefits from such activities.

The assessment of costs and benefits of small enterprise development projects in the form of rigorous "cost-benefit analysis" is difficult, but a number of approaches exist for measuring the cost-effectiveness of such projects. The present book discusses the evolution of SED evaluation and provides an insight into appropriate evaluation techniques for a diverse range of small enterprise support activities, including training, credit and technology. It brings together interesting and innovative examples from different parts of the world, and illustrates the authors' extensive experience of implementing SED projects world-wide.

In this book the reader will find information about tangible indicators of SED performance such as increased sales, higher profits and enhanced employment, as well as about measures of institutional sustainability for SED support agencies such as clients' willingness to pay, cost recovery and commercial viability. The book also touches on some less tangible measures of performance for SED projects, such as those covering the largely uncharted area of "quality of life", including the quality of housing, food, education and family welfare of project beneficiaries.

The book contains many references to programmes and projects in Bangladesh, India, Nepal, Pakistan and Sri Lanka. These illustrations complement the variety of approaches from Europe, Africa and the Americas, as well as from other countries in Asia and the Pacific.

I am grateful to my colleague, Gerry Finnegan, ILO-SAAT's Senior Specialist in Small Enterprise and Management Development, and his co-author, Malcolm Harper, an acknowledged expert in this field, for producing this very timely and valuable publication. The authors have combined their rich technical experience with their enthusiasm for promoting cost-effective approaches to small enterprise development.

This book would be most useful for those engaged in actively promoting small enterprise development, including: policy-makers and planners; donor agencies; national and international non-governmental organisations; employers' and workers' organisations; member-based associations of entrepreneurs or informal sector operatives; training institutions; banks and other lending institutions, technology centres, and academics and researchers.

March 1998   **A.S. Oberai**
Director, International Labour Organization
South Asia Multidisciplinary Advisory Team (ILO-SAAT)
New Delhi

Acknowledgements

We have both been working in small enterprises and small enterprise development for many years, perhaps too many. Our interest in evaluation originated from our earlier experiences in business, as well as from lecturing in the key business subjects of marketing and accounting. In the world of business, we were used to having our performance evaluated by our employees and our customers. In our lectures we promoted ideas about the importance of the customer, the relevance of market research and the significance of the "bottom line" in financial statements, where income from sales should exceed costs and expenses. We were therefore initially surprised and somewhat astonished, and later saddened, to find ourselves working in a field where success is frequently measured by the amount of money that has been spent, and not by what has been achieved.

We were pleased when we started our research for this book to find out that many of our colleagues in small enterprise development shared our frustration. Evaluation practice has improved significantly in recent years, but there are many people working in this field who are eager that their own work should be more rigorously and critically evaluated. They have been very willing to share their experiences and to encourage us to bring together this survey of evaluation approaches and techniques, in the hope that what is now the best practice will become universal. We acknowledge the contribution made by many colleagues in the SED field throughout the world. They have inspired us with their efforts to improve the impact of SED projects, and we hope that they will derive satisfaction and benefit from our findings and conclusions.

In particular, we would like to thank Michael Henriques, Chief Entrepreneurship and Management Development Branch, ILO Geneva for commissioning the original study which was circulated as a working paper entitled "Small Enterprise Development—Value for Money"; A.S. Oberai, Director, ILO-SAAT, New Delhi, for providing us with the necessary support to enable us to bring the book to a wider public; Godfried Ijsseling and Joni Musabayana; the New Delhi office of the Ford Foundation for making it possible for Malcolm Harper to give further time to work on the book; and to Patricia and Aislinn (18 months) for allowing Gerry Finnegan the time to undertake this publication. The library staff of the ILO in Geneva, of Cranfield University in England and of the Xavier Institute of Management in Bhubaneshwar have also been most helpful. Oxford & IBH, New Delhi, have as usual, shown themselves to be demanding and thus excellent publishers.

Malcolm Harper and Gerry Finnegan
Cranfield and New Delhi

List of Acronyms and Abbreviations

ADB	Asian Development Bank
ADEMI	Association for the Development of Microenterprises (Dominican Republic)
AKRSP	Aga Khan Rural Support Programme (Pakistan)
AMT	Achievement Motivation Training
BME	Benefit Monitoring and Evaluation
BRAC	Bangladesh Rural Advancement Committee
CARE	Cooperative for Assistance and Relief Everywhere Inc.
CDFI	Capiz Development Foundation Inc. (the Philippines)
CED	Centre for Entrepreneurship Development (India)
CEFE	Creation of Entrepreneurs, Formation of Enterprises (programme of GTZ)
CSEP	Craft and Small Enterprises Promotion Programme (Tanzania)
EDP	Entrepreneurship Development Programme
EDI	Entrepreneurship Development Institute (India)
FAO	Food and Agriculture Organisation (of UN)
FAS	Foras Aiseanna Saothair (The Training and Employment Authority, Ireland)
FIT	Farm Implements and Tools
GEP	Graduate Enterprise Programme
GTZ	German Agency for Technical Cooperation
IDA	International Development Agency

IDBI	Industrial Development Bank of India
IFAD	International Fund for Agriculture and Development
ILO	International Labour Organization
IRED	Innovation in Research and Development
ITDG	Intermediate Technology Development Group
IYB	Improve Your Business
M&E	Monitoring and Evaluation
MATCOM	Materials for Cooperative Management
MES	Monitoring and Evaluation System
MSE	Micro and Small Enterprises
NGO	Non-governmental Organisation
ODA	Overseas Development Administration (UK)
OECD	Organisation for Economic Cooperation and Development
Rs	Indian Rupees
SDI	Subsidy Dependence Index
SED	Small Enterprise Development
SEFCO	Small Enterprises Finance Company (Kenya)
SIDO	Small Industries Development Organisation (Tanzania)
SME	Small and Medium Enterprises
SYB	Start Your Business
UNDP	United Nations Development Programme
UNHCR	United Nations High Commission for Refugees
UNIDO	United Nations Industrial Development Organisation
$	United States Dollars
£	Pound Sterling

List of Boxes

Chapter 1

Introduction

The evaluation of small enterprise development programmes has long been neglected, or has at best only been carried out in occasional situations on an ad hoc basis. Several authors and researchers have noted this omission.

"Evaluation remains a forgotten tool among small enterprise practitioners.... This is a great tragedy."(Haggblade, 1992).

"It has never been shown that the net effect of subsidizing small firms is to create more wealth in the community" (Storey, 1987).

These may be extreme views, but Haggblade and Storey are recognised authorities in the enterprise development field in both less developed countries and the more industrialised countries of Europe, and they are not alone in their views. This publication is an attempt to remedy the situation and bring the need for evaluation to centre stage where it rightly belongs. In addition, many organisations involved in promoting small enterprise development are also discovering the importance of impact assessment. Therefore, the presentation of these ideas should be timely, and will we hope, be welcomed as part of a broad debate aimed at improving the impact and efficiency of development efforts.

Industrial development has a far longer history than small enterprise development, and in that regard there exists a tradition of nations, regions, districts and communities encouraging outsiders to establish industries within their midst in the form of inward investment, in order to contribute to employment and wealth generation.

In richer and poorer countries alike, the provision of assistance and encouragement to smaller enterprises, which are usually owned and operated by local people, is a more recent phenomenon. Indeed, it is only since the early 1970s that this has been a major item on the development agenda anywhere in the world. However, within this period of about twenty years, interest in small enterprises has grown to make it a very major part of development. Between 1980 and 1990, for instance, the World Bank sanctioned about three billion dollars in some five hundred credit lines for small enterprises. In the 1970s, the category hardly appeared in the classification of its projects. Bilateral donors have also become heavily involved. The United States has been a leader, as might have been expected from the important role which self-employment and small enterprises have played in its own economic development. Also, relatively smaller donors such as the Scandinavians have been pioneers in this field, usually in line with broader poverty alleviation and social development objectives. Small business is also seen as an important component of urban renewal. The Irish Government's aid programme, Irish Aid, includes microenterprise development activities in its urban upgrading programmes in Zambia, and the slum improvement projects in India which are funded by the United Kingdom also have a similar component. As will be seen later, this perceived connection between small enterprise promotion and broader social objectives has added to the complexities involved in evaluating the impact of small and micro-enterprise development support programmes.

As it has become less realistic to suppose that most people in developing countries — particularly the poorer sectors of the population — would be able to find jobs as waged employees in the formal or organised sector, so the emphasis of employment and industrial promotion programmes has changed. As examples from among the activities of United Nations' specialist agencies, the International Labour Organization (ILO) has extended its own interest from traditional employer-employee issues to those relating to the development of small enterprises, self-employment and the informal sector. Another UN specialist agency, the United Nations Industrial Development Organisation (UNIDO), has broadened the scope of its involvement in industrial promotion, and now supports the development of small-scale industries. The UN Food and

Agriculture Organisation (FAO), and latterly the International Fund for Agriculture and Development (IFAD), are also involved in the development of small-scale food processing and off-farm rural enterprises, and the United Nations High Commission for Refugees (UNHCR) has been involved in promoting self-employment activities for refugees.

In addition, there are many small enterprise development programmes being introduced in the "economies in transition" as they are sometimes called, in Eastern Europe, and Central and South-East Asia. These programmes have been developed in order to assist small businesses to contribute to the evolution of an enterprise culture and to provide a locally-based private sector, as well as to enable them to create jobs for their owners and employees, and provide much-needed goods and services to meet local demand.

National governments have also played a major part in small enterprise development, in some cases for much longer than foreign donors. In India, in particular, the Gandhian emphasis on village self-reliance which played such an important rolé in the independence movement, led to the evolution of a wide range of state and central government support programmes in favour of small-scale industries. The Khadi and Village Industries Development Commission (KVIDC) has for many years been promoting locally produced home-spun fabrics and other traditional utility and handicraft items and, some would argue, has been keeping these industries alive, thereby achieving valuable social, political and economic objectives.

The richer countries of Western Europe and North America are also heavily engaged in small enterprise development support activities, often in order to assist marginalised groups such as inner city minorities, young people, or unemployed or redundant workers to improve their economic and social position.

This broad range of governments and support agencies, as well as many others, has become involved in the field of Small Enterprise Development (SED) for a variety of reasons. Their objectives are frequently diverse, although they may use the same means to achieve them. This wide spectrum of agencies and their respective developmental objectives, may in part explain why standard evaluation criteria have not been formulated and why evaluation appears to have been assigned such a low priority.

Current Trends in Evaluation

Even if the standards of evaluation in this field had in the past been of the highest, it would still be appropriate to review this important issue since the purpose and nature of evaluation itself is also a matter of current debate. Small enterprise development necessarily and inevitably involves an element of social development, and it is clear that the designated participants, target groups or beneficiaries should have some role to play in any evaluation process, as well as in determining that which is being evaluated. As the ILO's guidelines state, evaluation should be "a collaborative effort rather than a judicial review" (ILO undated).

The Asian Development Bank (ADB) introduced its own system of benefit monitoring and evaluation (BME) in the early 1980s and it is applied to conventional economic activities, as well as to measure the achievement of social, environmental and institutional objectives (Samson, 1996). The BME approach consists of three sets of component activities:

- Preparation and analysis before the project of benchmark (baseline) information on individuals and groups affected by the project;
- Monitoring benefits received by intended beneficiaries;
- Evaluation of project impact three to five years after project completion.

However, BME implementation has not been as smooth as ADB would have liked, as it is still considered "time-consuming and too complex" (Samson, 1996). ADB is now attempting to integrate the BME approach into the logical framework so as to link it to the project design and management information systems of executing agencies.

Evaluation has traditionally been seen as a more or less ad hoc task which should take place at some point in the life of a project - frequently as a solitary, stand alone end-of-project procedure. Many authorities, such as Rubin (1995, p.114) and Marsden and Oakley (1990, p.35), now suggest that through proper use of client participation it should rather be seen as an integral part of the process which empowers rather than controls the actors. Participative evaluation, if misapplied, may do no more than provide an excuse for discussion, rather than becoming a meaningful activity in its own right. However, it can also enable those who may otherwise have been perceived as passive objects to take over the process of their own development, which is ultimately what any development project should aim to do.

In some quarters participation is often seen as the antithesis of a tough, hard-nosed commercial approach. However, more and more small enterprise development projects, particularly in the area of financial services, aim to develop the long-term capacity and sustainability of local institutions, to enable them to survive and grow on what they earn from fees or interest charges paid by their customers, rather than from the funds provided by donors. Such an evolution clearly requires that close contact be established with the project's emerging customers so as to identify their needs. Consequently, evaluation in these cases is much closer to market research than to the classic notion of project evaluation. Such client-centred evaluation must also be participative, since the future of the institution will depend on the wishes of its customers and not on donor priorities (Rhyne, 1994). This requires very different methods from the conventional tools of "shadow pricing" which impute real values for items such as labour, foreign exchange and other components. These tools are becoming less relevant since governments everywhere are removing price and subsidy distortions. Also, traditional financially-based applications of the "time value of money" and discounting procedures have become less acceptable universally, as increasing concerns about the wider long-term impact on the environment demonstrate the folly of undervaluing the future. In addition a problem arises in attempting to put a price tag on those factors which are not easily quantifiable.

Although many of these changes are beginning to take effect in current approaches to evaluation, it is still appropriate to recall some of the traditional evaluation techniques which are as relevant today as when they were first articulated. Freeman (1979) suggests three fundamental criteria by which any evaluation process should itself be "evaluated".

o Would other observers have come to the same conclusions with the same instruments?

- Does it show whether or not the same effects would have taken place without the intervention that is being evaluated?
- Have the results been achieved efficiently?

The Structure of the Book

We will start with an account of the breadth and variety of activities which come under the term "small enterprise development". A number of project evaluations are then reviewed in an attempt to assess the current "state of the art". As this is not the first publication to deal with the evaluation of small enterprise development, the review will be followed by a summary of other contributions to the field. Subsequently, the "who", "when" and "how" of evaluation are examined in more detail, with a particular emphasis on the choice of methods and measures suitable to the evaluation process.

Finally, an attempt is made to propose guidelines for anyone approaching the evaluation task. Of course we do not suggest that there is one universally applicable model which has merely to be applied in any set of circumstances. It should be pointed out, however, that there are several pitfalls to be avoided and issues which must be considered, particularly at the beginning of any project, which are worth summarising for the benefit of all practitioners. At the beginning of any project the sponsors, implementers and managers need to be clear about putting in place realistic and meaningful measures of evaluation which are achievable, in consonance with the project's objectives, and relevant to the target beneficiaries.

Chapter 2

What is Small Enterprise Development?

A large number of publications have devoted considerable space to attempts to define small enterprise. This has led to a bewildering plethora of sub-categories, such as microenterprise, medium enterprise, informal and modern enterprise, cottage industry, tiny enterprise, survival enterprise, and so on. It is not the purpose here to engage in a lengthy discussion on definitions. This book attempts to embrace the evaluation of any form of development and support activity which is intended to promote and assist an enterprise employing say less than one hundred people. The enterprises in question may be engaged in trade, industry or services, and they may be owned and managed by individuals or groups.

The breadth of types and sizes of enterprise demonstrates from the outset the complexity of the field, and the near impossibility of prescribing any universal form of evaluation. A development project which focuses on formal, high technology businesses is obviously very different from a project which aims to assist self-employed women in a refugee community. The only thing they may have in common is that both are concerned with "small enterprise". It is also clear that their evaluation will require different measurement methods, different time scales and different research and analytical skills.

The wide variety of services which are provided to develop these small enterprises, of whatever scale and type, also leads to a wide variety of evaluation problems. These support services — frequently divided into financial and non-financial services — may include loans and financial assistance, management and technical training, extension services, information, networking, consultancy, premises, incubator units, marketing, raw material supply assistance, and design services, whether for products, machinery or services. These may be provided independently or in a range of combinations. Depending on what each project provides, a different approach to evaluation will be required, even when all of the services are provided in an integrated way by one project.

Increasingly, support programmes are being designed to promote income-generation activities and micro and small enterprise development for women. Whether the approach adopted by the donor and implementing agency is one of mainstreaming women into core activities, or providing specialist assistance for women, the impact on the women needs to be considered and where possible measured. The evaluation of programmes which aim to promote women's self-employment, for instance, can include not only the direct economic benefits to women, but additional factors such as:

- The removal of barriers and constraints to women's enterprise in general;
- The simplification of administrative procedures;
- The identification of viable business opportunities;
- The increased availability of effective training;
- The development of networks of women entrepreneurs, and of government and non-government support agencies;
- The improvement of data collection on women's participation in small enterprises;
- The dissemination of information on business opportunities and support services;
- Increased acceptance by men of women being self-employed (ILO, 1995b).

It is dangerously easy, however, to confuse ends with means, and to seek to justify projects by increases in intermediate outputs such as training, publications or information which may or may not lead to the desired final results. The measurable indicators, in gender-related projects as in any others, must cover the achievement of final objectives.

Little work has been done on the environmental impact of small enterprises. Their production methods are often less efficient than those used by large firms to produce similar products, and small firms often cannot afford sophisticated pollution control equipment. On the other hand, the environmental impact of a number of small enterprises scattered over a wide area may be more diluted, and thus more able to be absorbed, than that of one large factory operating in one place. Programmes to promote the development of small manufacturing industries, or of small-scale transport firms, will probably be required in the future to include some dimensions of environmental impact in their evaluation.

In such cases criteria could be based on the enterprise's inputs (use of renewable resources and materials); processes (minimum damage to environment arising from production techniques and processes), and outputs such as the products and services produced, as well as ancillary aspects such as use and type of packaging materials.

Agencies which promote job creation through small enterprise development should be as concerned about the quality of employment generated, as they are about the quantity of the jobs. To this end the ILO has developed a programme on working conditions in small enterprises which has been successfully implemented in several locations (ILO, 1988). Known as Work Improvement in Small Enterprises (or WISE), the programme presents a large number of practical actions which small enterprises can take in order to reduce industrial accidents, generally improve the working environment, and at the same time enhance the productivity and profitability of the enterprises. The WISE training materials and manuals suggest a range of criteria which could be adopted in evaluating the quality of employment created by small and medium enterprise (SME) support activities.

The Variety of Project Objectives

Projects which use similar methods to assist similar types and sizes of business may nevertheless have very different objectives, such as:

- improve the supply of certain services to the community;
- reduce unemployment and/or underemployment;

- reduce poverty;
- socially empower a particular group of people.

These objectives are not mutually exclusive and some projects might aim to achieve all of them, but the differing primary objectives of each project will call for separate approaches to evaluation.

An increasing number of projects aim mainly to build local capacity in industry associations, financial or training institutions, or other bodies. There is often a trade-off between the rapid and efficient provision of services to small enterprises and the development of local capacity to continue to provide such services in the long term. Here again, the evaluation tasks and time-frames can be quite different.

The wide range of institutions which are engaged in small enterprise development imposes a further set of difficulties for the evaluator. Although institutional boundaries are becoming increasingly blurred, international and local non-government organisations (NGOs), private for-profit businesses, government departments and parastatal corporations themselves will have very different objectives. These quite legitimately will affect the objectives of their small enterprise development activities, and thus the way in which they should be evaluated.

Practitioners in every field claim that theirs is the most complex, and small enterprise development may be no different. The above summary of the variety which exists in this field may, however, serve as a warning against any tendency to look for standard approaches to evaluation, project design or other aspects of SED. What follows should be read in the light of this warning.

Chapter 3

The Evaluation of SED Training

While accepting that the current state of evaluation of small enterprise development leaves a lot to be desired, we intend to examine some examples of recent and not so recent evaluations in order to find out what has been done, what is being done, what can be learned from it, and what gaps remain.

Given the diversity of the SED field, it should prove more useful to examine evaluations of different projects of the same general type. Training has always occupied an important place in SED and it is often regarded as one of the most difficult forms of SED activity to evaluate. Training takes many different forms, even within the small enterprise field. Training can address the needs of people who may want to start their own businesses, of owners of existing businesses, of their employees or staff, or of institutions whose task it is to "develop" small enterprises. It can be offered at various levels of sophistication to a range of different categories of education and competence. Training can be provided on a very wide range of enterprise-related topics, such as entrepreneurship development programmes (or EDPs as they are commonly referred to), small business management, technical or skills-related training, contextual topics such as health and safety or environmental issues, or on processes such as lobbying and advocacy skills, networking skills, or the development of member-based organisations of entrepreneurs. In addition, the training can be aimed at either the entrepreneurs themselves, or at trainers and support workers who in turn train and assist entrepreneurs.

Evaluation of EDPs

One very specialised type of SED training which has a relatively long history is entrepreneurship development. It is appropriate to examine a number of evaluations of this particular form of enterprise development because it has been going on for more than thirty years, and because a number of significant evaluations of such programmes have been published. One of the authors has been involved in several of these programmes and their respective evaluation studies which are described below.

Entrepreneurship development is generally taken to mean training for people who want to start businesses, or for those who are already running them. It is usually separate from training in the technical skills required for a particular type of business, such as dressmaking or carpentry, and is additional to management subjects such as book-keeping or marketing. These topics may be included in entrepreneurship development, but the EDP courses usually include one form or another of personal development training.

These programmes may be aimed at enhancing certain desirable competencies, such as increasing the trainees' self-confidence and initiative. Most of these programmes originate from the pioneering work of David McClelland and his colleagues in southern India in the 1960s, long before small enterprise development became a mainstream industrial or developmental activity.

McClelland's Evaluation in India

It is appropriate to begin by looking at McClelland's work, because he was not only a pioneer in the field of entrepreneurship training, but also in its evaluation. Few subsequent evaluations have even attempted to attain the same degree of rigour as was applied in the evaluation of the original achievement motivation training (AMT) experiments in Kakinada and Vellore in India (McClelland and Winter, 1971). This evaluation calculated that the local training cost per new job created in trainees' businesses was Rs.183 (or about $25 in 1968 when the experiments took place), and that the trainees invested an average of $100 of additional capital in their businesses for every five dollars of training cost.

The investment made by the foreign donor in creating this local training capacity was estimated to be about $20,000, and although no attempt appears to have been made to estimate the overall return on this investment in terms of increased business profits or value added, the evaluation is unusual by today's standards in that it recognises the investment role of institutional capacity building. It demonstrates the very high value for money that this enhanced capacity could deliver, when compared with the efforts of similar government programmes in the same region.

McClelland went further and in an innovative approach attempted to measure the increase in economic activity in the affected communities by comparing the growth in their electricity consumption with that of similar towns where the training was not available — electricity consumption being seen as a "proxy" for industrial activity. It is instructive to compare the rigour of this evaluation of the initial experiment with later evaluations of similar programmes.

The GTZ Survey of EDP Evaluation

A survey of EDPs was carried out for the German Agency for Technical Co-operation (GTZ) in 1983 (Harper, 1984a). Of the fifty-three institutions which shared information about their approach to evaluation, nineteen were able to state how many of their trainees had started businesses after the training, but only a very small number of these had information about the quantity of jobs created or about the financial performance of the businesses. One exception was the Centre for Entrepreneurship Development in Ahmedabad, India, which was the nucleus of the very substantial entrepreneurship development "industry" which now operates in India. They were able to estimate that a total of 31,500 jobs had been created in the 2,550 businesses which their trainees had started.

The ILO ENT/MAN Survey

A more comprehensive survey of 107 institutions offering training in the field of entrepreneurship and enterprise development was published by the ILO in 1992 (ILO ENT/MAN, 1992a). This survey obtained a wide range of information about the content and scale of the training programmes, and it also included a question about evaluation methods. Thirty per cent of the respondents did not answer the question on evaluation, while a further 5 per cent stated that they carried out some evaluation but gave no further details.

Of those that did provide information, 22 per cent stated that they gave questionnaires to trainees in the classroom at the end of the training, while a further 7 per cent administered questionnaires in the field some time after the training. A further five per cent judged success by subsequent recruitment figures, 17 per cent counted the numbers of businesses which had been started by trainees, and only 14 per cent attempted to use measures such as job creation, investment or profits.

Box 3.1: Methods used in evaluation (ILO survey)

22%	Questionnaires to trainees at the end of training
17%	Numbers of businesses started by trainees
14%	Measures of job creation, enterprise investment or profits
7%	Post-training questionnaires in the field
5%	Subsequent course recruitment figures
5%	Unspecified evaluation methods
30%	No information given
100%	TOTAL

The ODA Study in India

A further survey of EDP evaluation methods was carried out for the British Overseas Development Administration (ODA) in 1991 (Harper and Mahajan, 1992), and had as its focus the Indian experience. There were some 700 institutions in India offering EDPs, but the main purpose of this survey was to identify those which exemplified best practice in evaluation procedures. The directors of twenty-eight of what were the best-regarded programmes were asked to provide details of their evaluation methods.

Twenty-five stated that their main method of evaluation was to count the number of businesses which their trainees start, and the majority also used measures such as the number of trainees completing satisfactory business plans or having loan applications approved, as well as asking trainees to fill in an evaluation form at the end of the course. Five stated that they went further than this, and used more detailed measures such as job creation, turnover, profits and investment. Six also claimed to make use of control groups and some form of cost-benefit analysis. As can be seen, some techniques and measures were rather basic (such as end of course evaluations), while others were more sophisticated, including the use of control groups and cost-benefit analysis.

Box 3.2: *Evaluation criteria adopted by Indian entrepreneurship development organisations*

- Number of businesses started by trainees
- Number of trainees completing satisfactory business plans
- Number of trainees having loan applications approved
- Completing evaluation form at end of EDP training
- Comparison of results with control groups of untrained businesses
- Cost-benefit analysis
- Use of detailed measures, including:
  — Job creation
  — Turnover
  — Profits
  — Investment

Of the 28 respondents, the seven who appeared to be evaluating their programmes more rigorously than the others were visited by the researchers in order to find out more about their evaluation methods. However, although their efforts to carry out evaluation were laudable, in general the results were disappointing. They seemed to have taken the question about "cost-benefit analysis" and applied it only to their own institutional costing systems. They also understood the term "control group" to mean unsuccessful course applicants rather than a matched sample of untrained people. None of them was attempting, as a matter of routine to do more than to count the numbers of business start-ups their trainees had achieved.

It is interesting to note that these Indian programmes are not part of any donor-assisted projects which have to be routinely evaluated by their sponsors, but are run in an ongoing manner by government and non-governmental organisations, just like any other training institution. Since their sponsors' objectives are to promote new enterprise, their failure to carry out more wide-ranging and comprehensive evaluation is perhaps not unreasonable. As a consequence, it leaves all manner of unanswered questions about the institutions and the enterprises which were created as a result of the EDP training, such as the long-term sustainability and viability of the enterprises, or the degree to which the institutions' programmes are delivering value for money.

The study did uncover a few isolated examples of one-off rigorous quantitative evaluations of EDPs, and the Centre for Entrepreneurship Development (CED) in Ahmedabad, India, was again shown to be a leader in this regard. In a group discussion their staff stated that they calculated the average training cost per business start-up to be around Rs.10,000 (c. $300 at this time), since each course cost about Rs.100,000 ($3,000) and about one third of the 25 trainees started new businesses.

All-India data which had been gathered for the study apparently shows that the average investment in a new business is about Rs.100,000, and CED had found that their trainees typically started with about Rs.10,000 less than the average. Since their studies have also shown that trainees' businesses fare better than average in terms of employment generation, survival, profits and growth, this suggests that the investment in training was a good one which showed positive results.

This ODA study on Indian EDPs also attempted its own modest ex-post evaluation study. This was to determine whether the practical difficulties of data availability which respondents had mentioned were such as to make it impractical even to try to use before-and-after financial information, as well as control groups. This small study compared approximately matched samples of 64 trained and 66 untrained entrepreneurs in Rajasthan and Assam. The additional profits earned by the businesses owned by the "treatment" group represented an average 35 per cent return on the training investment. This figure was arrived at in spite of using very conservative estimates for the applicable time-frame for calculating resulting increases in profits. The trained entrepreneurs achieved significantly better figures for factors such as growth in turnover, trainees' own earnings and employee numbers.

The sample was small and, given the limited scope of the study, it was not possible to disaggregate the effects of the various additional inputs which the trained entrepreneurs would have enjoyed, such as privileged access to finance or power connections. Nevertheless, the study showed that the results can at least be said to demonstrate that, (a) rigorous evaluation of this type of small enterprise development training is possible, and (b) in this case at least the training was probably a good investment of public resources (Harper and Mahajan, 1992).

Evaluation Study by Industrial Development Bank of India

A further study of a 'Block Adoption Programme' in an Indian sub-district, carried out by the Industrial Development Bank of India (IDBI), showed that the average training cost per job created was about Rs.4,600 (or $150), and that it resulted in average annual earnings per trainee of Rs.6,300 (or $210) (Acharya, 1990, pp. 63-66). This represents an annual return on the training investment of 140 per cent (calculated as the annual earnings as a percentage of the training costs per job), but such a calculation takes no account of other development inputs not directly related to the cost of training, nor does it compare the results to those of a control group of untrained businesses. Similar data were provided for a programme in Assam (India), where self-employed trainees were said to be earning a minimum of Rs.3,600 per year, while the training cost was some Rs.4,000 each, thus demonstrating a return on the training investment of 90 per cent.

Piecemeal data and findings of this sort are obviously subject to many caveats. However, it is certainly true that in some areas at least, such as the tribal areas in Assam, people would have been most unlikely to start their own businesses without the stimulus and assistance of the training programme. In deciding to start their own businesses they would presumably have foregone some earnings from other sources. This also shows that control groups are not always relevant yardsticks in every situation.

The Study by Entrepreneurship Development Institute of India

Since the ODA study was carried out, the Entrepreneurship Development Institute of India (EDI-I) has since carried out major evaluations of its own and other institutions' EDPs (Awasthi and Sebastian, 1992 and 1996), drawing in part on the methodology which was evolved in the ODA study described above. The study identifies what are said to be the four main objectives of this form of EDP training: (i) increase the supply of new entrepreneurs; (ii) diversify the base of enterprise ownership by developing what are called "first generation entrepreneurs" from communities which have not traditionally been active in this field; (iii) reduce unemployment; and (iv) improve the performance of businesses.

In the EDI-I study, a whole range of qualitative and quantitative variables are examined, including the impact (a) on the trainees themselves; (b) on society at large; (c) on policy-makers and government, and (d) on the international arena.

As indicated earlier, in India the promotion and management of EDPs is a substantial industry in its own right, employing many thousands of people, and one measure of the impact on government, as well as outside India, can also be seen in terms of the funding agencies' willingness to finance increasing numbers of programmes.

A survey of 865 trainees was undertaken, drawn from the participants in 145 programmes conducted in eighteen different states. This large sample was used to obtain data on aspects where comparison with untrained people was not relevant, such as their start-up rates, opinions about the training, and so on. More detailed information was obtained from a smaller group of 67 enterprises, and this was compared with data from a control group of 89 businesses. The members of the control group were in the same industries with similar locations and initial investments, and had been started within three to four months of the treatment group's enterprises. The survey data showed that the members of the control group were generally older than the treatment group, but had similar levels of education and prior experience, and they came from similar family backgrounds.

The rates of growth in sales, profits, investment and employment were all found to be significantly higher for the trained (treatment) group as opposed to the control group. The annual return on the training investment of Rs.10,723 (or approximately $360) per business started, as measured by the higher profits earned by trained entrepreneurs, was estimated to be 27 per cent. The investment multiple of the training was calculated to be 27.5:1, indicating that the trained entrepreneurs invested 27.5 times the cost of the training intervention. Furthermore, each enterprise which was started by a trainee created an average of five jobs in addition to employing the owner, so that the training cost per job came to Rs.1,795 (or approximately $60 at the current rate of exchange).

Most of the programmes were sponsored by development finance institutions, and the study points out that only 7.6 per cent of businesses owned by trained entrepreneurs "fell sick", to use the Indian terminology, which signifies that they defaulted on their loans. The average sickness figure for all small industries is 11.3 per cent, and the EDI-I researchers calculate that the reduction in losses of interest and principal alone in the case of the trainees almost covers the total direct cost of training.

It is possible to find fault with some aspects of this evaluation, and some of the data — such as that for job creation — was not incremental since the figures for employment do not appear to have been compared with those for the control group. The study itself might have been more credible if it had been carried out by an independent outside institution, instead of by EDI-I itself, whose very survival might have been linked with the results.

The results are nevertheless comparable with those obtained in the earlier ODA study carried out by independent observers. Furthermore, the Indian EDP evaluation experience demonstrates not only that EDPs seem to be effective and efficient, but also — and for the purposes of this publication, more importantly — that it is possible to evaluate non-financial small enterprise development programmes in a rigorous and quantitative way.

Entrepreneurship Development in the Philippines

In 1983 an impact assessment was carried out on entrepreneurship development programmes implemented by the University of the Philippines — Institute for Small Scale Industries (UP-ISSI), the foremost EDP agency in the Philippines (UP-ISSI, undated). In general the study concluded that:

- The EDP was an effective method of economic development and employment generation.
- The EDP hastened the dispersal of small economic activities and contributed to the distribution of income generating activities to the regions.
- The EDP was an economic form of employment generation.
- It is possible to inculcate entrepreneurial qualities, traits, skills, managerial values and orientation to adults through a well-organised study and training programme, provided that the individual possesses the necessary basic traits.

More specifically, the following outcomes emerged from the UP-ISSI impact study.

- The EDP influenced participants in either setting up a new business or in expanding an existing business. Fifty-one per cent of respondents said they were able to expand their business after the EDP compared to 43 per cent prior to attendance.
- Businesses operated by EDP graduates had a higher lifespan of 7.5 years compared to the national figure of 6.0 years.

However, although many programmes and projects endeavour to carry out some form of evaluation of their activities, the findings are often presented in an impressionistic manner, thus not doing justice to the effort which went into the evaluation process. As an example, the Programme of Entrepreneurship Development of SENA — Division for Entrepreneurship development in Bogota, Colombia (SENA, undated), indicated that from 4,314 enterprises assisted in 1990, the enterprises achieved the following:

- Sounder management training;
- Greater ability to cope strategically with changes in the environment;
- Solution of specific technical problems;
- Training of middle management staff;
- Improved management of functional areas;
- Improved productivity.

Rather than being described as an evaluation of the Colombian programme, these "achievements" could have been used as a basis for obtaining more objective information with which to quantify the development and progress made by the enterprises.

The CEFE Global Evaluation

The GTZ "Competency-based Economies through Formation of Enterprise" or "Creation of Entrepreneurs, Formation of Enterprises" (CEFE) programme is in some ways an international variant of the Indian EDP approach. It was started in Nepal in the early 1980s as part of an integrated community development programme in Bhaktapur, a town in the Kathmandu valley. It has now reached some seventy countries through an extensive network of affiliates and accredited trainers, and it is vigorously and effectively promoted by a small group from GTZ headquarters, supported by an enthusiastic team of trainers and motivators throughout the world.

The components of the training programme are similar to the Indian EDP model, which has itself been substantially modified since the original approach to enterprise development was initiated by McClelland. There is also considerable scope within the CEFE approach for local variations, depending on the particular project to which CEFE is attached, the specified target groups and local needs, and the inclinations and priorities of the local personnel.

A comprehensive evaluation of the CEFE programme was carried out recently. Unlike the two Indian studies referred to above, the full text of the CEFE evaluation is not in the public domain, but a summary has been produced (Kolshorn, 1994) in the CEFE in-house magazine, which is published from Frankfurt to keep the

CEFE "family" in touch with one another's activities and to spread the CEFE gospel more widely.

The evaluation team, consisting of three researchers, visited five countries and surveyed a total of 156 CEFE trainees, and interviewed a large number of CEFE staff and associates, and other informed authorities. They found that 38.5 per cent of CEFE trainees had started their businesses, and a number of others were still in the process of getting started; 44 per cent definitely had not started and did not appear likely to do so. Each business was found to have created an average of 4.5 new jobs after training, and this figure, like that for the proportion who started, is remarkably similar to the findings in the Indian studies.

The in-house magazine summary is particularly interesting because the writer, who is the head of CEFE, inserted his own comments in italics at certain points. These are quite revealing of the attitudes which often arise among project promoters concerning dispassionate evaluations of their work. The article points out, for instance, that although the average figure for start-ups is only 38.5 per cent, which is high by the standards of most EDPs, a figure as high as 90 per cent has been achieved in one country.

The summary states that the evaluators felt that CEFE was "too expensive". Unlike the Indian evaluations this is not quantified, and we are not told how much money has been spent on the programme. Therefore, it is not possible to make any assessment of the cost-effectiveness of the CEFE programme. The article also indicated that CEFE is a pilot project and that its costs have been high because they include initial development costs which will not be repeated.

More recently, the impact of the CEFE programme in Nepal was revisited by Tomecko and Kolshorn (1996) and they stated that CEFE's entrepreneurship development programmes had an average start-up rate of sixty per cent. They state that the "direct cost per training course was $1,000". In addition, they cite "later evaluations in 1996 estimated that the project had created 4,866 new businesses and 129,500 jobs at an average cost per job of $84".

The CEFE methods, it is stated, aim at two levels of sustainability.

i) Sustainability for the participants of training courses. This is a function of:

- how well the training was conducted;
- the involvement of complementary host institutions;
- the follow-up provided by the host executing agency.

ii) Sustainability for the national and regional implementing institutions, which is dependent on:

- the correct choice of the host agency;
- the development of qualified trainers;
- effective follow-up from international sponsors of CEFE;
- the proper use of monitoring and evaluation systems.

The findings on the CEFE programme raise an important issue concerning such innovative approaches which have required considerable investment in development costs. CEFE and the ILO's Improve Your Business (IYB) programme as described below are two examples of this. It would seem that in the case of CEFE, a genuine pilot programme would long since have been discontinued as a "pilot" if it had proved to be successful and was being replicated on a large scale in many countries. Otherwise, if found unsuccessful, it should have been stopped. These comments, however, need to be seen in a broader sense since, like many contemporary enterprise development projects, CEFE aims to build local capacity, and not just to provide training to potential entrepreneurs.

It would be reasonable to assume that if GTZ ceased to fund CEFE, at least some of the affiliated institutions and trainers would continue their work, possibly with local or client funding. Therefore, some part of the large expenditure by the German government can legitimately be considered an investment in developing training capacity, rather than an expense of training. The CEFE case simply underscores the complexities involved in attempting to carry out SED evaluations, as well as trying to separate out the direct and indirect impacts of SED programmes. It is an issue which we will return to later.

It is apparent that the total costs incurred in the development and management of the whole CEFE programme, as funded by the donor, and the costs of trainer training in particular, are many times higher than their Indian equivalents, as measured by the ODA and EDI-I studies. This may explain why the GTZ figures are not in the public domain. From the standpoint of promoting the objective evaluation and cost-effectiveness of programmes such as these, it is somewhat unfortunate that it is not possible to compare the costs of this very comprehensive programme with its Indian or other international or nationally-based equivalents.

Early Evaluations of CEFE in Nepal

An early evaluation of a small pilot extension project for existing small businesses in Nepal (part of the origins of CEFE), attempted to compare local costs and benefits and assess the return on the investment of the foreign donor (Harper, 1984b, p.185). The figures achieved by the clients were compared with those of a roughly comparable control group, and the local costs of the extension service inputs per enterprise were estimated to be $470. The additional annual turnover per business, less the cost of purchased materials, which gives some measure of the added value or increase in economic activity, was almost three times this figure. The additional profits were almost twice the training cost. This demonstrated that it would have been a very sound investment for the clients to pay the full local costs themselves, had they been asked to do so. In this earlier study, value for money and cost-effectiveness were clearly demonstrated, and the long-term viability and sustainability of the approach seemed assured.

The annual return on the estimated GTZ investment of some $70,000 was 13 per cent in terms of additional value added, and 8 per cent in terms of enterprise profits. This estimate assumed that the improvements would be maintained over a longer time span, but it was also based on the assumption that the local institutional capacity would continue to provide similar services without any additional foreign investment. As often happens, it appears that the results of the evaluation were not used as a basis for deciding on the devolution of the financing, management and expansion of the pilot approach to the local partner. This activity has subsequently evolved into a major ongoing project, which is still expatriate-managed and largely foreign-funded some twenty years later.

Recent Evaluations of CEFE in Sri Lanka

The CEFE model has also been implemented in Sri Lanka through the Sri Lanka Business Development Centre (SLBDC) and in recent years serious efforts have been made to assess the impact and cost-effectiveness of these programmes, and to assess the prospects for sustainability. In Sri Lanka, as well as in other countries of the sub-region such as Nepal and Bhutan, there has been a tradition of trainees receiving a stipend or allowance while attending training programmes. For this reason charging a fee for the training, which is a first step towards sustainability, is very difficult in these countries, particularly if the training agency is linked to government in any way. Interestingly, in Bhutan a significant step has been taken by the Entrepreneurship Promotion Centre in convincing the government that stipends should not be paid to trainees on its Comprehensive Entrepreneurship Course. Fees may follow later. In Sri Lanka there is no tradition of small-scale entrepreneurs paying for training and, as a consequence the donor has to foot the bill (Reichert and Herath, 1996a). It is not surprising in these circumstances that no genuine commercial market for this form of training has evolved in Sri Lanka, or indeed elsewhere. It would only be possible to evaluate the training by the standard of clients' willingness to pay if the stipends were eliminated and participants were asked to pay a significant part of the cost. This seems unlikely at the present time.

In the evaluation of CEFE programmes carried out in Sri Lanka for the Ratnapura Integrated Rural Development Programme (IRDP) during 1994–95, it was found that 51 out of the 75 CEFE trainees had gone into business or had implemented their expansion or restructuring plans within 12–18 months of training, thereby giving a "success" rate of 68 per cent (Bandaranayake et al., 1996). In addition, "the number of employment opportunities created under the programmes is 136". The report documents various systematic steps and procedures that the SLBDC-CEFE staff went through to follow up on the trainees in order to determine their post-training status. Follow-up concentrated on finding out whether the trainees were in business or not, or had expanded or not, as well as on counting the "employment opportunities created".

The Sri Lanka-German CEFE programme started its own monitoring and evaluation system in 1995, based on approaches being developed by CEFE in other countries. This system was presented at the CEFE International Conference which was held in Cape Town in September 1996 (Reichert and Herath, 1996b). The monitoring and evaluation (M&E) system introduced by CEFE in Sri Lanka is comprised of three M&E questionnaires: (1) the participant's survey which includes information on the participant; business background and experience and the business idea, and detailed information on the status of up to three businesses operated by the entrepreneur; (2) the details of the entrepreneur's business plans; and (3) a business plan implementation survey. Each of these questionnaires is very comprehensive and requires considerable time to complete, both for the entrepreneur and the business adviser. The responses are provided before training, after training, and on three or four follow-up visits over a twelve-month period.

Evaluation of the Graduate Enterprise Programme (GEP), Cranfield (UK)

The Cranfield Graduate Enterprise Programme (GEP), which ran from 1984 until 1990, was one component in the United Kingdom government's programme of new enterprise development initiatives in the 1980s. Its objective was to enable more graduates to start their own businesses. An intensive and rather expensive training programme was provided to a small number of carefully selected graduates, and it was also hoped that the graduate community in general would be encouraged by their example to consider more seriously self-employment as an option (Brown, 1995).

In order to attract good applicants and, more importantly, to spread the message of self-employment as a viable career option for graduates, the programme was organised in three stages. Half-day awareness workshops were held at college campuses throughout the country, attended by some 4,000 students each year. About 1,000 of these graduates then progressed to attend two-day appreciation workshops, from which about 20 were invited to participate in the GEP training itself. The GEP occupied twenty training days, spread over a twelve-week period. The two preliminary workshops were designed to be "stand alone" events (like the self-selection filters used in some entrepreneurship development programmes). They were designed to be of value to the participants in helping them in making decisions about their future, as well as holding out the possibility of leading to the subsequent stage if they so wished and were selected.

At the national level during the six years when the programme was offered the number of graduates entering self-employment increased by 93 per cent, while the number of graduates entering the job market only increased by 38 per cent. There were clearly many reasons for this, including the general evolution of an enterprise culture and rapidly growing unemployment, but it seems reasonable to ascribe at least some part of this increase to the widely publicised examples of the GEP graduates as role models. This view is strengthened by the fact that in 1991, when the programme was stopped, the number of graduates becoming self-employed actually fell by four per cent. Therefore, the role and contribution of such pilot programmes, expensive though they may be, also need to be assessed in terms of the promotional function which they serve in providing high visibility for a particular activity and approach, and in ensuring that this is brought to the attention of a significantly large number of the target group.

The Cranfield School of Management was the pilot provider of the GEP (which was subsequently introduced to other universities and polytechnics in the UK), and an extensive data-base was set up to monitor the fortunes of the people who had been trained. The whole endeavour was assessed in April 1992, two years after the conclusion of the last of the programmes. The total cost of the six programmes was estimated to be £970,000 (or $1,550,000). Sales and profitability figures for GEP trainees were obtained for the first three years of their trading, or less if they had started more recently.

The businesses that had been established by trainees were found to have achieved cumulative profits of some £1,350,000 ($2,160,000) on sales of over ten times that amount. It might be assumed that these annual levels of sales and profits would continue and even increase, if the growth of the successful surviving businesses exceeded the reduction caused by the inevitable closure of some others. In this way the results could be viewed as a continuing return on the government's investment in GEP training, rather than as a one-off result of the six years of training.

In addition, it could be argued that this was a reasonable return on the government's investment, even in the narrowly defined sense of taxation yield. An average tax of 25 per cent of the additional annual profits resulting from the training, of say £500,000, would have provided an annual return on the government's investment in new enterprise training of 12 per cent (based on the cumulative profits of £1,350,000 indicated above).

The evaluation of the GEP also demonstrated that the businesses had created 231 full-time and 22 part-time jobs, including the jobs of the owners of the businesses. The cost per job was therefore about £4,000 (or $5,500), which was substantially more than the figure claimed by many other government enterprise development programmes with a much lower profile than the GEP. The increase in investment amounted to three times the training cost, half of which was by the entrepreneurs themselves and half was raised from the banks.

The highly selective recruitment process meant that there was a large number of rejected applicants of almost as high a calibre as those who took the complete course. Indeed, many of those rejected had also demonstrated the same level of commitment by going through the two preliminary workshops and applying for the third component of the programme. Therefore, it was possible to assemble a control group whose members had a similar profile to those who received training on the GEP.

About one-third of the control group had started businesses in spite of their rejection from the GEP, and 89 per cent of the remainder intended to do so in the next five to ten years. In contrast, over sixty per cent of the GEP trainees had started and were still in business at the time of the study. One can speculate that a major effect of the GEP may, therefore, have been not so much to increase the proportion of graduates who start their own businesses, but to bring forward the timing of start-up by five years or so.

It was interesting to note that the financial results achieved by those members of the control group who were willing to share them were significantly better than those for the businesses started by the GEP trainees. Sales were about twice as high. In the first year, profits were much lower, perhaps representing a longer period of learning on-the-job which the GEP trainees were able to avoid, but thereafter the profits were around twice those of the GEP trainees.

These figures can be interpreted in various ways, but they are dramatically different from the Indian EDP data which show a significantly better performance for trained as opposed to untrained entrepreneurs. It might be argued that the stimulus of rejection was a powerful incentive to do well, or that excessive training was dysfunctional in that it created a group climate in which even marginally motivated trainees felt obliged to proceed and start in business. It could also be argued that similar people who were not part of the GEP group were not put under this pressure to perform and establish their own enterprises. Alternatively, the short and intensive two-day training input may be sufficient, or even preferable, for the truly committed person.

Whatever the conclusions, clearly the results of this evaluation would have prompted a complete reassessment of the GEP had it been continued. It is significant to note, however, that this evaluation study was not undertaken at the behest of the government sponsors of the programme. By the time the results were available the whole system of funding and support provided by the British Government for this type of initiative had changed. This raises the issue of the differences in the time horizons established to meet certain political objectives, as opposed to the objectives of the programme implementers, or indeed those of the programme beneficiaries.

For the last 20 years Cranfield has also run international courses for the staff of small enterprise development agencies, and the evaluation of these courses also raises the issue of sponsor interest in evaluation. While it is difficult to evaluate the impact of a short training course on a banker or community development worker, it is still more difficult to measure its impact on the clients and target beneficiaries of his or her organisation. However, the high cost of foreign-based training means that it is necessary to evaluate the training in some way. The Enterprise Development Centre at Cranfield attempted such an evaluation by asking each participant to commit himself or herself to a specific action to be undertaken on his or her return home as a result of the training, and then trying to follow up and find out whether this had been successfully implemented. The results have been mixed and not wholly conclusive (Harper, 1996), but it may be significant that only on one occasion has a sponsor has ever shown any interest in the evaluation process, and that was only at the personal level and for a very brief period.

The ILO's "Improve Your Business" Programme (IYB)

The ILO's IYB programme is not dissimilar to the German CEFE project, or indeed to the EDP system in India, in that it is based on a franchise system whereby trainers are trained in a particular approach. Thereafter they are permitted to offer training under the approved label of the IYB, under the supervision of one of the ILO's IYB focal point institutions in almost 80 countries where the IYB material has been adopted fairly extensively.

The IYB originated as printed training materials in small business management, adapted from a Swedish original. It was initially planned that the training material would be widely distributed and would itself lead to an increase in the quality and quantity of small business training.

It was found for a number of reasons that development of the material alone was not sufficient and the programme slowly evolved into a small business training programme which made use of the training material but was delivered by the programme staff. More trainer training led eventually to the present franchise approach, and the growing reputation of the training system and the demonstrated quality of the trainers has now reached the point where trainers, in Zimbabwe at any rate, are able to charge the full cost for their training (IYB, 1995). The IYB programme is itself becoming a successful business. This is something which is often hoped for small enterprise development projects, but is so rarely achieved in practice.

Since the early 1990s, there have been several significant modifications and improvements made to the original IYB approach through the introduction of an IYB Basics programme in southern and eastern Africa, as well as a new Start Your Business (SYB) approach which originated in Fiji and has also been further developed in Africa. In addition, a sectoral adaptation of IYB has been developed for the small-scale construction industry in west Africa, known as Improve Your Construction Business (IYCB). The predominant emphasis of the present programme and of the IYB evaluation studies that are covered here tends to be in Africa, where the programme operates in thirteen countries, training around 4,000 entrepreneurs every year.

The IYB's main coordination office in Harare has produced a very comprehensive Monitoring and Evaluation (M&E) Kit (ILO, 1994) which includes cards to be completed by trainees themselves, as well as by the trainers, before, during and after the training. These cards provide a sustained record of trainee progress, which can be used for individual counselling and for further training needs assessment, and are thus a valuable tool for the trainers. The trainers are encouraged to keep the cards up to date, not primarily to provide evaluation data for the project, but to help them to serve their clients more effectively. Each trainer reports to a training co-ordinator who makes routine checks on the cards in order to maintain the quality of service delivery, as in any well-run franchise operation.

The clients themselves are also involved in providing the data, once again not to assist in project evaluation, but to enable them to monitor and evaluate their own progress and the results of the investment of their own time and money in the IYB training. This of course is what evaluation should eventually become, as and when donor or government subsidised projects evolve into commercially viable businesses. It is hoped that the IYB M&E kit will facilitate this conversion process in Zimbabwe and elsewhere. This systematic approach provides a model which can be adopted, modified or adapted in other situations. However, it should be kept in mind that the cost and effort involved in evaluation should not outweigh its benefits

The IYB programme has also been subject to a number of more traditional evaluation studies in various countries. A study of the impact of the programme in Kenya (ILO, 1987a) used as one indicator the trainees' expressed willingness to pay for future courses. This showed that trainees who had been on one course would be willing to pay more than twice as much for a further course, although it should be noted that the report then went on to recommend a higher level of subsidy rather than greater reliance on client fees. The study also obtained a limited amount of data from a control group of fifteen untrained business owners, but found no significant differences in their performance compared to the IYB trainees. The overall conclusion was that "a few entrepreneurs have increased their productivity or profitability because they participated in the IYB course", but there was no attempt to quantify this or to relate it to the total cost of the courses, for which no figure was mentioned in the report.

A 1992 evaluation of the "Improve your construction business" (IYCB) project in Ghana, a sector-specific offshoot of the IYB (ILO, 1992b), is perhaps more typical of the standard of earlier evaluations and of earlier assessments of field performance. It gives the number of people who were trained, but only mentions in passing that they were not able to apply what they had learned.

A more recent evaluation of the IYB programme was completed in 1994 on behalf of the Swedish government who continue to be the main sponsor of the programme. This study (Forss and Bjern, 1994) states that since its establishment in 1977 the project has cost around ninety million kroner (or nearly $13 million at the present rate of exchange), and 25,000 people have been trained in Africa alone.

This study was based on responses to a survey carried out with a sample of trainees, but in the process no attempt was made either to compare the results of trainees with non-trained business owners, or to compare the costs of the programme as a whole to the estimated benefits to the businesses. The evaluation includes some brief case studies of presumably typical clients. This demonstrates that statistical data alone are not sufficient to give outside readers a feel for the nature of what is being evaluated in SED programmes such as the IYB. From the point of view of objective and scientific research, the use of case studies can be deceptive if they are only chosen from the most successful clients. However, the trend in social science research towards more qualitative methodologies (such as the use of case studies and case histories) should inform small enterprise evaluation methods, which are after all social science investigations of a specialised kind.

This IYB study points out that the value of the benefits which the more successful trainees claim to have achieved as a result of the training would exceed the total local costs of the training within "a year or two". This was stated, even though only 25 per cent of the trainees stated that they had benefited in this way. Such a conclusion suggests that, with better selection of trainees, the training could have been a very good investment for the majority of the trainees and therefore a good business proposition for the franchised training institutions.

The study is more critical of the lack of efficiency of the IYB programme and approach, in that it took seventeen years to reach its present position of being able to demonstrate tangible benefits. It states that "at present, the benefits to the individual entrepreneur fully justify the cost of the programme", but this relates to today's local costs only, and not to the present rate of support from ILO offices in Harare, the Geneva headquarters and the network of ILO's multidisciplinary teams (MDTs) which are also involved in IYB support activities. Still less consideration was given to the substantial investment in the 17-year development process.

During 1996 ILO carried out a survey of its Improve Your Business and Start Your Business programmes in many countries, as well as consolidating the findings of earlier evaluations of the programme (ILO, 1996a). With the development of a family of IYB approaches, including the new IYB Basics and the Start Your Business (SYB) programme, the ILO's package has been renamed as SIYB — Start and Improve Your Business.

The original IYB programme appears to be an extreme case of heavy investment in the development of capacity of both the entrepreneurs themselves, as well as of the implementing partner organisations. This can only be evaluated in terms of the value to clients of improved small business management training approaches by the trained trainers, and of strengthened institutions. In contrast, the promoters of many micro-enterprise credit projects can claim some element of institutional sustainability, as the IYB trainers in Zimbabwe are beginning to do. Yet it is important to take full account of all the earlier investment that has been necessary to achieve this position before making a final judgement.

ILO's MATCOM Programme

The ILO's IYB approach was not dissimilar to that adopted at around the same time by the ILO Materials for Co-operative Management programme (MATCOM), which produced a wide range of training guides and self-study manuals in the management of agricultural and other co-operatives. The MATCOM material was successfully introduced to a large number of specialised co-operative training institutions and, after substantial local modification, has been used in the training of over a million co-operative managers, particularly in China, Indonesia and India, but also in many countries in Africa, the Caribbean and the South Pacific (Taimni, 1994).

The MATCOM programme was wound up several years ago, since it was perceived as having achieved its objectives. It has not been formally evaluated, since the very wide diffusion and local ownership, and the local adaptation and translation of the training concepts and manuals, means that most of the trainers who use it, and certainly many of those who are trained with its assistance, are unaware of its origins.

This demonstrates the difficulty of carrying out a conclusive evaluation of indirect support initiatives, such as the development of institutional capacity or the production of training material. Perhaps the most convincing evidence of the success of such projects and programmes is that those whose capacities they have enhanced know nothing of them! This clearly complicates the complex task of evaluation, which is already difficult because the links between the training material and improved business performance are in themselves so tenuous and difficult to demonstrate or substantiate.

Chapter 4

The Evaluation of Technology Programmes

The development and diffusion of technologies that are "appropriate" for application in developing countries with a low level of infrastructure, is another major form of small enterprise development. It can be argued that Schumacher's impassioned advocacy of intermediate technology in his seminal work "Small is Beautiful" (Schumacher, 1973) played a major role in the evolution of the whole small enterprise development movement throughout the world.

Technology-based programmes, like others in the field of small enterprise development, do not lend themselves to any single standard or means of measurement because the aims and objectives of each programme can differ significantly. For example, programmes to promote better and more efficient stoves can create jobs for the stove-makers, they can save time and money in their applications (such as cooking, heating or small-scale production processes), they can improve health conditions for their users, and they can have significant environmental implications by reducing the demand for timber and pressure on forests. These programmes may also contribute to significant modifications in attitudes among policy makers, which in turn can lead to major changes in industrial policy whose ultimate impact goes far beyond the project's benefits to the few hundred people who gain directly from the stove programme intervention.

This same situation can be applied just as well to other types of small enterprise development programmes. Yet there is a tendency for many of those in the appropriate technology movement to resist efforts to measure direct benefits or to relate these to costs. This may be because of the broader but indirect benefits that the programme promoters expect to be achieved, in the form of environmental improvements and policy reform.

The Intermediate Technology Development Group (ITDG)

The ITDG, which was itself established by Schumacher and can be said to be the original from which all similar institutions have sprung, is now heavily involved in a large number of individual development projects through its increasingly autonomous country offices. The 1992 triennial review of ITDG's work (Economic Planning Associates, 1992) commented that information on individual project costs was not always available, as cost data were not collected automatically for each project, but only gathered at the request of certain donors. However, costs were sometimes known at the field level through the systematic efforts of some project managers.

The Kenya stove project was one for which locally estimated cost data were available. From this information it was estimated that the project earned an internal rate of return of 30 per cent, based on the initial investment and assuming that the benefits continued for a seven year period. The cost per job created can be calculated as between $3,500 and $4,500, without making any additional allowance for environmental or other indirect benefits. This figure can be compared with the target cost per job of $1,800 which is used by Appropriate Technology International, the American counterpart of ITDG.

The ITDG reviewers also calculated some sample cost-benefit figures, and found that the cost per job created in small-scale mining in Zimbabwe was about $4,300, while the cost per job in a small-scale building development project in the same country was between $11,500 and $23,000. In this latter case, however, it was expected that three times as many jobs would eventually result from the project, so that the cost per job would be lower if spread over the additional jobs created.

ITDG's project proposal documents which are used to present projects both internally and to external donors, include a very detailed calculation of costs as a basis for the funding request, and in some cases they make quite specific estimates of the expected numbers of beneficiaries. It is estimated, for instance, that it will cost $180,000 to train 100 women in Zimbabwe in improved methods of small-scale mining, and $28,000 to create between 30 and 40 jobs in a hand-made paper workshop in Bangladesh. But the review documents themselves make no attempt to relate these two figures or to draw cross-comparisons. The costs appear to be presented in order to secure funding, and cost-effectiveness is not seen as a major issue, although the necessary data appears to be available.

As was reported for the CEFE and IYB small enterprise development programmes, the costs do not include the international overheads incurred by ITDG itself. There is a case for arguing that such long-term and less direct *costs* should be ignored because the *benefit* assessment also omits any calculation of the value of the wider dissemination of information and additional long-term attitudinal changes. It is nevertheless paradoxical that while most small business training manuals, a number of which are published by the ITDG itself, stress that small business people must include overheads in calculating their costs — and thus in determining their prices — major international organisations such as ITDG do not include headquarters overheads in the financial assessment of their own activities.

The reviewers conclude that "there remains a tendency to ignore measurements of efficiency and effectiveness". It is clear that many ITDG projects, like those of several other appropriate technology or SED organisations, do represent very good value for money. This tendency to "ignore measurements of efficiency and effectiveness", and the failure to include all the costs (including HQ overheads) or to relate the costs to the benefits, can be attributed to many factors. It appears to arise, not so much from fear of exposure or scrutiny, as from a fundamentally non-economic view of development — a belief that benefits cannot or should not be measured exclusively in financial terms.

Reference is made elsewhere to the changes in recent years in NGO field staff's perceptions of evaluation. However, in spite of the widespread adoption by ITDG and other agencies of the logical framework, with its focus on measurable indicators of achievement, there remains some reluctance to adopt a totally business-like approach, where every item of expenditure must be rigorously related to the returns that are expected to result from it. Robert McNamara's views may not be fashionable today, particularly in NGO circles, but his statement on quantification is still worth quoting in this context: "Not to quantify what can be quantified is only to be content with something less than the full range of reason ... to argue that some phenomena transcend precise measurement — which is true enough — is no excuse for neglecting the arduous task of carefully analysing what CAN be measured." (McNamara, 1968).

This may be expected from organisations which owe their origin and still claim allegiance to a "movement", such as appropriate technology. The prevailing attitudes to evaluation tend to be part of the tension which is created between the sub-contracting or project "selling" activities on which organisations such as ITDG, other NGOs and international agencies must increasingly depend, and the ideology of the NGOs' founders and the ideals of at least some of their present staff.

Other Technology Programmes

The recently established ILO/TOOL programme, whose complete title is "Promotion of appropriate tools and implements for the agriculture and food processing sectors through local intermediaries", but which is generally referred to as "Farm implements and tools" (or FIT), has commissioned a number of short evaluation studies on a range of specific project activities. The studies demonstrate that a more quantitative approach to evaluation is possible, which can also presumably serve as a useful aid for day-to-day management purposes within the FIT projects themselves.

Exchange Visit Programme by FIT in Kenya

One FIT programme in Kenya consisted of a one-day workshop for small enterprise owners, followed by individual five-day attachments for the entrepreneurs to larger firms operating the same type of business. The total local cost of the programme was estimated to be about $10 a day (Hileman, 1994), not including the costs incurred by the collaborating institution or the FIT programme's overheads. The evaluators state that "the entire cost of the program has not been made available", so their omission of any international HQ overheads is perhaps more understandable than in the case of ITDG. Nevertheless they did make a very thorough attempt to assess the benefits that the entrepreneurs derived from the programme.

The participants paid the equivalent of $20 for the workshop and attachment. They were reluctant to do this before participating in the programme, but many said afterwards that they would be willing to pay $40 for a further similar exposure. This demonstrates the common situation where entrepreneurs are obviously initially reluctant to pay a substantial sum for a totally unfamiliar service. This means that at first the service may have to be offered free or at a heavily subsidised fee. Thereafter, clients may be willing to pay all or a large part of the cost once the tangible benefits have been demonstrated and experienced.

This factor can be used as an indicator of the possible economic viability and sustainability of continuing a service, as well as a means of evaluating clients' attitudes towards an experiment. In one situation clients of a pilot type of small enterprise extension service were asked after six months of free service whether they would be willing to pay for its continuation (Harper, 1974), and about 70 per cent said that they would. Although it was decided not to continue the project's service in the same area, at least one of the service's trainee extension staff took advantage of this known willingness to pay and operated as an individual small business consultant after the completion of the experiment.

The FIT evaluators also attempted to assess the impact of the attachment component. Clients claimed to have created 38 new jobs as a result of what they had learned. They also claimed to have achieved substantial increases in sales and profits through lessons learnt on the programme, such as the adoption of new maintenance and operation techniques, new marketing ideas, new customer contacts, and improved management and self-confidence. An attempt was also made to interview a sample of the clients' customers to determine whether they had noticed any improvement in the services which they had received. Although no attempt was made to compare these results with any control group, it became quite clear that the improvements stated were far more dramatic than would have been experienced during the same period by a similar group of businesses without the benefit of the exposure programme.

In attempting to measure the impact of the technology exchanges, FIT carried out its assessment based on three major aspects: technology gains, marketing improvements and management improvements.

Box 4.1: The impact of technology exchanges

Technology gains were measured in terms of:

- Information on Suppliers
- Repair Skills
- Sources of Spare Parts
- Information on Tools
- New Product Designs and Technology

Marketing improvements were measured in terms of:

- Marketing Ideas
- New Business Contacts
- Improved Communications with Customers
- Information on New Markets
- New Customers

Management improvements were measured in terms of:

- Increased Self-confidence
- Record-keeping
- Employee Relations
- Specific Management Technology

Brokering Programme by FIT (Kenya)

A further evaluation was carried out on another FIT programme in Kenya involving a two-day "brokering" activity designed to enable small-scale entrepreneurs to learn from one another (Craig and Cerone, 1994). This was estimated to have cost a total of $3,030, or $89 per participant, although it is not clear whether all local and international overheads were included in this figure. The evaluators state that while they were not able to assess the financial value of the benefits in order to compare them with this cost, they were able to identify a large number of improvements in clients' businesses such as the introduction of new products and equipment, new markets and distribution channels, and the creation of an additional four full-time and three part-time jobs. Clients also expressed their willingness to pay for further workshops of the same kind.

This evaluation also attempted to measure changes in sales and profits. Interestingly, over half the businesses experienced a reduced level of sales after the workshop, and a quarter reported lower profits. However, since the increases more than covered the reductions, the total figures for sales and profits for all 34 participants taken together were substantially higher. A net monthly increase in profits of $274 seemed to be a reasonable return on the total investment of approximately $3,000. This conclusion begs the question of whether the changes actually resulted from the workshop. In order to make a more rigorous assessment of the value of such workshops in the future, Promotion of Rural Initiatives and Development Enterprises (PRIDE) — FIT's collaborating institution in Kenya — is attempting to locate a control group so as to isolate the impact of project interventions.

Other Evaluation Exercises carried out by FIT

More general FIT evaluation documents (Tanburn, 1995; Wesselink, 1995a) identify the importance of customer demand as an indicator of success. This should originate from the customers of the client enterprises in the form of demand for the new products developed under the programme. In turn, this is translated into demand from enterprises for support services, so that the local institutional partners will eventually demand support services from the FIT programme in order to enhance their ability to provide these services. The FIT documents summarise a wide variety of indicators, as well as their respective advantages and disadvantages. They also demonstrate the value of evaluation as a means of promoting client ownership of the programme. The conclusion seems to be that the "qualitative objective impact on MSE activity" is the best, but not the only indicator to use in programme evaluation.

Evaluation of Incubator Units

Small industry estates have generally lost favour as a form of small enterprise development, although industrial estates for all sizes of business are still widely promoted as part of regional development programmes. However, specialist "business incubators" where small firms, particularly in high technology fields, are intensively assisted for a limited period, are quite common. In a recent assessment of the Business Incubator approach (Lalkaka and Bishop, 1996), the impact of a range of programmes in industrialising and industrialised countries was reported. A "model" incubator programme in Michigan, USA, indicated an average cost for each job created of $1,642, with 4 jobs created on graduation from the incubator unit, and an average of two further jobs created subsequently. The study also examined incubator units in China, the Czech Republic, Mexico, Poland and Turkey, and used criteria such as enterprise creation (e.g. in the Czech Republic 17 units have helped to create 440 enterprises); employment creation (e.g. in Poland's 19 incubators, some 238 businesses have created 1,670 jobs); costs per job (the various studies showed an average cost of $835 for one person-year of employment).

In Mexico the scheme is assessed in order to monitor and evaluate the incubator units' activities and the following aspects are measured:

- Number of tenants;
- Self-sufficiency of both incubator and tenants;
- Average number of years for graduation from units;
- Income of tenant companies.

An additional aspect, the links between academia and industry — which is common to many incubator programmes — is also assessed using the following measures:

- Instances of technology transfer to new companies;
- Number of researchers, students, or teachers involved in technology-business enterprises;
- Numbers of patents and other means of capitalising technologies.

Summary

In summary there are several ways of measuring the impact of technology development programmes, and these are shown in Box 4.2.

Box 4.2: Appropriate impact measures for technology development

Environmental improvements
Health improvements
Policy changes
 	
Customer reactions
 	
Enterprises' willingness to pay
New designs developed
New designs adopted by enterprises
New designs sold
Enterprises' sales and profits
 	
Job creation
Cost per job:
    ITDG: $ 3,500–$ 4,500 stoves, Kenya;
        $ 4,300 mining, Zimbabwe
        $ 11,500–$ 23,000 building, Zimbabwe
   ATI target: $ 1,800

Chapter 5

Other Evaluation Experiences

In the previous chapters a number of evaluation studies of enterprise training and technology development programmes have been examined. Although these programmes are comprised of several different components, including classroom sessions on various aspects of small business management, behavioural training aimed at personal development, as well as individual counselling and follow-up and extension services, the input was quite brief and evaluation is relatively straightforward. In relation to these interventions, the question that needs to be examined is "Did the training or other activity achieve the stated objectives, and at what cost?".

Integrated development programmes pose more complex evaluation problems, since they cover a wide range of services and every client is likely to have enjoyed a different mix of services, possibly over a long period of time. In addition, the programme objectives may also be more diverse. International organisations such as the ILO have implemented a number of such programmes, as have many NGOs. A large number of these activities are run as projects with a fixed-term duration, rather than as the regular activities of continuing institutions. As a consequence, it may be that evaluation is viewed as a bureaucratic requirement rather than as a routine management tool.

We provide a brief review of a selection of evaluations of such integrated programmes as run by the ILO, the World Bank, donor agencies and NGOs. This should enable comparison with the studies of the EDP, small enterprise development and technology training programmes reviewed earlier, as well as comparing the approaches of various international agencies to the design and implementation of evaluation procedures.

Evaluation of ILO Programmes

The ILO's guidelines for evaluation (ILO, 1996b) suggest several aspects which should be covered in an evaluation study of any activity. These include: relevance; efficiency; effectiveness; sustainability; identification of alternative strategies in achieving the same objectives; an appraisal of unanticipated effects; causality; validity of design in present circumstances; and findings, conclusions and recommendations arising from the activity.

These guidelines point out that the present methodology for assessing efficiency is imperfect, since there is no definitive way of objectively comparing inputs with outputs. A cursory examination of a number of evaluations of ILO small enterprise development projects suggests that most evaluators have opted not to make any attempt at such comparisons. As befits an international organisation whose primary concern is with employment, job creation is the main focus of much of ILO's technical cooperation development activity (ILO, 1995c). However, it is easier to assess the number of jobs that may have been created, than to evaluate the efficiency and effectiveness of the projects that are said to have created them.

A summary assessment of various ILO activities was produced in 1987, in which the results of the evaluations of 37 ILO rural small enterprise development projects were drawn together (ILO, 1987b). In five cases, the data provided related exclusively to measures for assessing project inputs, such as numbers of people trained. Others gave some information about the numbers of enterprises reached or assisted. Although the document gives the cost of the project in every case, the data are not presented in a way that makes it possible to compare the costs with the benefits and results, and the summaries of the evaluation studies do not attempt to relate the two variables in any way.

Closer reading of some individual ILO evaluation reports reveals a wider range of approaches to the process of evaluation itself. The 1993 evaluation of a self-employment project in Indonesia (Sweeting, 1993) presents an interesting comparison between the cost per enterprise and cost per job generated through a university-run and an NGO-run programme. The two programmes were directed at two distinct markets, being the educated unemployed and poorer less-educated people respectively. The university programme cost $116 per job and $218 per enterprise, while the equivalent figures for the NGO programme were $42 per job and $125 per enterprise. These figures were only for the training part of the project, and did not include the cost of capital or other resources that were provided. However, they do demonstrate the lower costs that frequently occur in programmes implemented by NGOs, as opposed to those carried out by more formal institutions, as well as showing the higher benefit/cost ratio often demonstrated through enterprise assistance to poorer and presumably more needy people.

A 1985 evaluation of an ILO project in West Africa to train bankers to extend more credit to small enterprises (ILO, 1989) gives details of the numbers of courses and numbers of bankers who were trained, but makes no mention of whether or not they actually lent more money to the intended beneficiaries. Similarly, a project to assist refugees in Lesotho was criticised by the external evaluator because the small number of relevant enterprises meant that the small business adviser was seriously underemployed (ILO, 1987b). The Lesotho study states that the adviser only worked with eighteen businesses, employing an average of seven people each (being 126 in total), and that the total cost was $340,000. It is left to the reader to conclude whether or not the benefits to the clients are likely to have justified the expense. An evaluation of a project to assist refugees to start or expand businesses in various parts of Sudan is similarly silent on the costs of what was achieved (ILO, 1990).

It is worth noting that enterprise development programmes for refugees face their own sets of problems, as the target group is subject to an unusual amount of transience and uncertainty in relation to their business operations, their inputs/supplies and their markets. Evaluation of SED programmes for refugees will inevitably focus on a wide range of performance criteria, over and above enterprise performance.

Like the Indonesian study referred to above, a more recent study of a small enterprise and informal sector promotion project in Cambodia (Ferrera, 1994) compared the relative promotion costs per business for formal and informal enterprises. It also went further and provided some data on the increases in income that were achieved, stating that a daily income increase of $1.50 was achieved, against the total cost of the programme of $500. Once again the reader is left to calculate an approximate benefit/cost ratio. The concepts of return on donor investment or value for money do not seem to have concerned the evaluation process, but much of the necessary data has at least been made available.

World Bank Evaluation Studies

A study on behalf of the World Bank (Levitzky, 1986) reviewed the Bank's small enterprise projects in fourteen different countries. No attempt appears to have been made in any of the numerous projects to assess whether they actually created additional jobs or businesses, or to relate the total cost of technical assistance or the subsidy elements in International Development Agency (IDA) loans to the overall benefits achieved. It may be that Stern's general comment about evaluation practices of the World Bank also applies in the case: "Serious cost-benefit analysis takes time and analytical resources of quality and is therefore seen as both managerially irritating and costly" (Stern 1994, p.83).

Another study of World Bank experience between 1980 and 1990 gives the impressive total of 600,000 jobs created, at an average cost worldwide of $4,675 per job (Webster, 1990). The average figure for Africa was $9,850, but this was balanced by the lower figure of $3,171 in Asia. These figures relate to the investment per job rather than to the costs incurred by the Bank itself. The paper also states in a general way that many of the technical assistance components failed to achieve their objectives, and that loan recoveries were also very poor in many cases. The total costs in terms of technical assistance, as well as the transaction costs less interest income of the on-lending financial institutions, would therefore presumably be high. Nevertheless, one would hope that these additional costs were not as high as the total investment costs given above.

In general, the World Bank projects aim to create employment through the development of small enterprises themselves, but also — and perhaps more importantly — to strengthen the financial and technical assistance institutions serving small businesses so that they will provide more effective and efficient services to this sector in the future. They also aim to correct the market imperfections that tend to restrict small borrowers' access to credit. It is clearly difficult to comprehensively evaluate how well such wide-ranging objectives of this kind have been achieved, but the Bank's own evaluations have apparently concluded that in over half the cases at least two of the three main objectives have been substantially achieved. Approximately one-third of their projects have failed to achieve any of their main goals. These individual project evaluations do not appear to have focussed so much on the important issues of value for money, the effectiveness of the participating institutions, or the reasons for failure or success.

It can be argued that project evaluations of the kind referred to above, which have the specific objective of directly assisting small enterprises, should at least make some attempt to relate the costs to the benefits and to calculate the resulting "value for money" obtained. Undoubtedly the task becomes more difficult when the project aims to develop institutional capacity, and particularly where the institution itself does not have the same commercial orientation as that of a bank or other potentially self-sustaining organisation.

This could be said for a member-based organisation such as an entrepreneurs' or employers' association. The ILO is involved in a number of such institution-building initiatives (ILO, 1986), some of which are implemented through one of the ILO's tripartite constituents, the national employers' organisations. Unless the objective is to create a self-sustaining enterprise development department within the organisation, the evaluation of such activities must necessarily be less direct and less precise than the simple assessment of cost per job or cost per enterprise created. Measures such as increases in numbers of paid-up members, fees earned from services, new services offered, or reduced dependence on subsidy can be used to evaluate such institution-building projects, but it must not be forgotten that these are only means to the ultimate end of more sustainable employment in the businesses served by the institutions.

Evaluations of Other Programmes

NGOs have traditionally been concerned with social welfare and community development, but it is only relatively recently that they have become involved in small enterprise development activities. This has happened for many reasons, but especially as it became clear that disadvantaged people could only become genuinely empowered and independent if they were able to increase their incomes. This has required many NGOs to reassess their objectives and for their staff to critically reflect on their own views and attitudes. In many cases the staff may have had something of an "anti-business ideology" where only community enterprises or cooperative businesses were acceptable, and where profit-making or the employment of one person by another almost necessarily implied exploitation.

It has been a common occurrence at Cranfield (UK) for staff of NGOs attending enterprise development courses to be asked on arrival to express their views on a number of issues relating to possible conflicts between traditional views of charity and the development of business. Among other questions, they are asked to state whether they agree or disagree with the following statement: "It is impossible to evaluate our work in enterprise development for the poor in terms of financial costs and benefits; human development cannot be valued in dollars and cents." In 1987, when this initial attitude and training needs survey was first used, the majority of NGO participants agreed wholeheartedly with this statement. Eight years later, only a small minority agreed, but this view has clearly affected the evaluation methods and processes still being used by many NGOs.

NGO Programmes in Latin America and the Philippines

An account of the impact of some Latin-American experiences in promoting microenterprise development through solidarity groups (Otero, 1989a) summarises two examples of approaches to evaluation from Colombia and the Dominican Republic. These cases illustrate the emphasis which NGOs place on social as well as economic indicators. One evaluation demonstrates the new paradigm that has arisen from the growing realisation of the importance of institutional sustainability. If the support project itself becomes a self-sustaining institution based on income from its earnings, the issue of cost-benefit analysis ceases to be relevant since there is no longer any external subsidy involved.

The second study (Otero 1989b, pp.79-81) describes the evaluation methods employed by twelve NGOs working with solidarity groups in Colombia. They used a common "impact evaluation format" in order to facilitate the comparison of results from one project to another. Field staff survey a sample of clients every six months, and their investigations cover the most critical areas of the enterprises' activities, including income, employment, savings, the business, community and programme participation, quality of life, group solidarity and attitude changes. This explicitly recognises the integration of the business with the household economy, since all the indicators — except those relating to the enterprise itself — relate to the family.

A factor such as "Quality of Life" is obviously difficult to assess on an objective basis, but in certain situations it can be more important than quantitative indicators such as income or savings, or "softer" indicators like participation or group solidarity. Indeed, some of these are no more than a means to this somewhat intangible end. However, the actual questions that are used to measure quality of life can be relatively easy to answer. In some examples families were asked whether as a result of the programme they ate better now and whether their housing had improved. They were also asked to judge whether they lived better in a general sense, and to state the main reason for any improvement that they believed had occurred.

The results differed from one programme to another, but all participants were in agreement that their food situation had improved more significantly than their housing, and that the main reason for the improvement was higher income from their microenterprises. These microenterprises were of course the target of the credit, training and other support services provided by the projects. This approach to evaluation shows that impact can actually be measured by programme staff as part of their working routine, and that clients' own responses to carefully designed questions can be used to provide an approximate but regular indication of social as well as economic impact.

A rather different example taken from the Dominican Republic shows that quantitative data can be routinely collected by project staff as part of their continuing self-appraisal, and in attempting to effect improvements in their own work. This information, once collected, can then also be used as a basis for periodic external evaluation. The staff of the ADEMI programme in Santo Domingo, Dominican Republic, regularly collected client data relating to fixed assets, sales, savings, earnings and job creation, and changes were monitored from month to month. The data for 1986 showed that client earnings had increased by between ten and twenty per cent during the year, while the numbers employed in client enterprises increased by around twenty-five per cent. Sales increased somewhat more rapidly, but the most dramatic increase was in savings, which increased for different groups, albeit from a low base, by between five and sixty times during the year.

This increase in savings also had a direct impact on the sustainability of the programme itself, since client savings provided an increasing proportion of the loan fund for the credit component, thus reducing the dependence on donor funds or on more expensive sources of borrowing. The evaluation does not therefore include any benefit/cost assessment, since the objective was to evolve towards a self-sustaining institution. We will examine other micro-finance schemes in more depth in Chapter 6.

In the Philippines an impact evaluation was carried out by the Capiz Development Foundation Inc. (CDFI) to assess the benefits from its integrated project to develop rural enterprises and promote entrepreneurship among rural women and young people. It was shown that the project had "a tremendous impact on the quality of life of the beneficiaries and of the CDFI as a development institution" (UP-ISSI, undated mimeograph). Excerpts from the impact evaluation carried out eighteen months after project implementation indicated that:

● As many as 87.5 per cent of the beneficiaries felt that the project was able to provide them with a decent and reliable source of income through the various livelihood projects they undertook.

- There was a marked improvement in the health and nutrition of the beneficiaries' dependents. In addition, children's educational needs were taken care of as a result of the beneficiaries' projects.
- At the community level, a substantial number of unemployed were absorbed by the beneficiaries' projects. One enterprise employed three persons, in addition to the entrepreneur's children.
- The CDFI was able to gain new experience and skills in implementing enterprise and entrepreneurship development programmes.

Another evaluation, of the Norwegian Missionary Alliance Programme for Employment Creation through Small Enterprise Promotion and Employment Exchange in La Paz, Bolivia, shows that NGOs can be very rigorous in their evaluation methods (Westborg Konsult, 1996). The programme provides credit, training and other support, and the additional annual earnings achieved by client enterprises were found to exceed the cost of the programme by a factor of 45 times. The cost calculation included an allowance for capital erosion through inflation, and the benefits were adjusted to take account of the opportunity cost of labour. Not unreasonably, the evaluation recommended that the programme should be extended to new areas. There was apparently no need for further outside support for its activities in the existing areas, because clients were said to be paying fees and interest which cover the full cost of the operations.

CARE's Evaluation Framework

CARE, which is one of the largest and arguably more professional of the international NGOs, has for some years been involved in enterprise development through a range of programmes, including credit and other inputs. The CARE evaluation framework for small enterprise development projects (CARE, 1995) proposes four levels of impact assessment: the beneficiaries, the local economy, the institutions and the services themselves. These are presented within the matrix of the logical framework approach to project planning.

By introducing the four levels of impact assessment at the project design stage, from the outset all stakeholders are made aware of the need for evaluation in order to determine the project's impact.

The emphasis of the evaluation at the beneficiary level is very much on economic change, such as income, fixed asset and savings accumulation, and changes in labour time. In relation to the impact on the local economy, upstream and downstream effects on suppliers and consumers are also taken into account, as is the development of related infrastructure such as market facilities, roads and information.

At the institutional level the main focus appears to be on CARE's own projects and country offices, since CARE has, at least until recently, concentrated on the development and growth of its own activities rather than on their evolution into viable institutions from which CARE itself can withdraw. This demonstrates the implicit conflict that can arise on the one hand between the growth and prosperity of donor organisations and their international contractors such as CARE, and on the other the objective of developing autonomous local institutions.

This is relevant not only at the institutional level but also at the level of the staff of the international institution, whether they are expatriate or local. Most people prefer the relative security, high pay and status of a job with an international non-government organisation, or indeed any other type of international organisation, to a position in a newly established local institution. Consequently project and individual staff evaluation parameters have to be adapted to reflect this factor in local institutional development.

Aga Khan Rural Support Programme (AKRSP) in Pakistan

The AKRSP in the northern areas of Pakistan is generally considered to be one of the most successful integrated rural development programmes. In recognition of this the Operations Evaluation Department of the World Bank, whose main task is to evaluate the Bank's own programmes, took the unusual step of evaluating the AKRSP's work (World Bank Operations Evaluation Department, 1990), even though the World Bank itself was not a donor to AKRSP.

This programme is not only concerned with small enterprise development. Its main emphasis is on the evolution of community groups with a primary focus on economic activities, such as the construction of infrastructure projects, irrigation and forestry, savings and credit, and agricultural production and marketing.

The World Bank study used a large number of different impact measures. These included volumes of inputs, such as fertiliser and new varieties of seeds that were supplied; sales and operating costs of marketing organisations which AKRSP had helped to establish; number of people trained, and adoptions and sources of new technologies. In an attempt to isolate the effects of the programme, incomes and new input usage by households which were members of active village organisations were also compared with those of households whose organisations were inactive.

The study also attempted to calculate annual programme costs per beneficiary household, which were estimated to total about $500 over a twelve-year period. This figure is stated to be "relatively modest" when compared with equivalent World Bank project expenditures per household of around twice that figure, incurred over a period of six to eight years. However, no attempt was made to compare the AKRSP cost with the slightly higher incomes per household which were found for members of active village organisations.

In general, NGO evaluation studies appear to cover a wider range of impact measures than those of other organisations, but the issue of value for money still often tends to be neglected, even when the necessary data seem to have already been obtained as part of the study. This is perhaps surprising since one of the main advantages of NGOs is, or at least used to be, their lower cost structure because of their use of volunteer and semi-volunteer staff. Therefore, most NGOs ought to be in a relatively strong position to be able to demonstrate reasonable value for money in comparison to international or donor-funded projects.

The SIDO/GTZ Crafts and Small Enterprises Promotion Programme (CSEP), Tanzania

The GTZ has been assisting the Small Industry Development Organisation (SIDO) in implementing the Crafts and Small Enterprises Promotion (CSEP) programme in Tanzania since 1992. This is an innovative attempt to provide services to informal urban businesses through their own self-help organisations. By early 1997, the project had worked with some 200 self-help organisations in Dar es Salaam, which had around 12,000 member enterprises. Initial attempts were also being made to extend the service to other urban areas, through the regional offices of the Small Industry Development Organisation (SIDO).

The Project operates through extension workers who offer a range of "sub-projects" to the self-help organisations. These cover aspects such as how to set up and manage a savings and credit scheme, how to draft and maintain a workable constitution, how to manage common services to members such as security, cleaning or toilet facilities and, above all, how to protect the members from harassment by the municipal authorities or others who wish to take over the sites where the members operate. In Dar es Salaam, informal businesses are frequently displaced by official "clean-up" interventions, and this threat is the main reason why the members have established their self-help organisations.

The self-help organisations pay a fee for each "sub-project" which is substantial for them even though it only covers less than 10 per cent of the Project's costs, and the demand for additional services from existing client organisations, as well as from new ones, suggests that the services are appreciated.

The Project is, however, not content to rely only on clients' willingness to pay as an indicator of its achievements. No "sub-project" is considered to be completed until the members have expressed their satisfaction with it, and the Project has also designed what is known as the "Membership Satisfaction Analysis", where members are asked in a carefully structured way to give their opinions about various aspects of their organisation. This involves group meetings where members place numbered cards in labelled pockets in a form of secret ballot. In this way, it is intended to ensure that individual opinions are not swayed by an articulate minority, and it also enables illiterate people to express their opinions. However, this is both complex and time-consuming for Project staff and 'their clients, but it does offer members a valuable opportunity to evaluate their own organisation, as well as monitoring the extent to which the Project's services have increased members' satisfaction. The results of this analysis are collated and compared over time, and the Project only "counts" or includes organisations where 75 per cent or more of the members are satisfied with the achievement of its purpose. The analysis is carried out when the Project starts to work with a group, and after conclusion of a "sub-project" the improvement in the group's satisfaction can also be measured.

Numerous other indicators are also maintained, such as the number of different services offered by organisations to their members — the average number has doubled for the organisations which have been serviced by the Project. Since strengthening the organisations is only a means towards the end of assisting their members, however, the Project's planning matrix also included the target of increasing members' individual incomes by 20 per cent more than what they might have expected if their self-help organisation had not been serviced by the Project.

A study was undertaken in December 1995 to ascertain whethe. this target had been achieved (Kobb, 1995). Data were obtained from 224 members of groups which the Project had served, and a control group of 112 unserviced business people. The median daily income of the treated sample was found to be Tanzanian shilling 3,000 (about $5) while that of the control group was about $4.50. There was a wide range of responses within each group, however, such that the omission of a small number of extreme cases could radically affect the final result.

The conclusion was that the study was itself a "dubious exercise". Micro-entrepreneurs, whose groups opted for the Project's services might well have been better off beforehand, so their higher incomes could not confidently be attributed to the Project, and "treated" group members might be more accurate in their assessment of their own income than the members of the control group. The margin of error for each response was also found to be very high, because of different ways in which the business people understood the question. Each interview lasted 45 minutes, but this did not remove the chance of different interpretations, and inaccuracies are inherent in the process of obtaining income data from informal business people who keep no records.

The Project nevertheless persisted in its attempt to find out what effect, if any, it had had on members' incomes, and commissioned a further study in December 1996, with similar sample sizes (Kobb, 1996). Some methodological changes were made, but the results were if anything less conclusive. The median of the "treated" businesses' incomes was only 3.4 per cent higher than that of the control group. This suggested that the effect of the Project during the year had been to reduce the margin of difference, and if only seven extreme cases were excluded it could be shown that the incomes of the control group were higher than those of the treated group.

The author concluded, as he had the previous year, that a wide range of quite possibly spurious and conflicting conclusions could be drawn from the data and that the results could not be used for serious decision-making.

The Project's objectives also included the indicator that at least half of the treated businesses should have at least one more business than the control group. The main objection to using increases in income as an indicator is the practical difficulty of measurement, which these studies reaffirm. Some might argue that increases in the numbers of businesses owned by individuals is associated with a tendency to operate at the margins or to over-diversify, rather than being a desirable or intended feature. However, the Project included this indicator as a measure of capital accumulation and growth. In the event, both the 1995 and the 1996 studies failed to come up with any more conclusive evidence for this indicator than for income increases.

The author of the studies suggested that clients' willingness to pay was a more meaningful indicator and that if it was felt that this was insufficient, because the present fees only cover about 7 per cent of the costs, experiments should be undertaken to judge its value by gradually increasing the fees until clients say "no" (Kobb, 1996). He suggested that clients might even be asked whether or not they would prefer to receive a cash sum which was equivalent to the subsidy, instead of the subsidised service. The Project has not taken up this option.

In future, the service will be have to be delivered without the benefit of a German subsidy, and it is becoming clear that the costs of delivery can be substantially reduced and client fees can be increased. It is unlikely, but not impossible, that the fees will ever cover the full cost, but as the proportion of subsidy falls the validity of "willingness to pay" as an indicator of achievement will presumably rise.

The attempts which the SIDO/GTZ Project have made to measure their impact on the self-help organisations and on their members go far beyond what most small enterprise development projects do, and they demonstrate quite clearly the practical difficulties of obtaining objective data which might enable one to answer the question, "Is this Project delivering value for money?". The market-driven philosophy which informs the SIDO/GTZ Project is consistent with the view that clients' willingness to pay a significant price for a service is perhaps the most valuable indicator of its worth, and it is also of course the easiest to monitor. However, the issue of value for money, or cost-benefit, remains unresolved.

Chapter 6

The Evaluation of Micro-Finance Programmes

Some SED programmes attempt to offer a wide range of support services to clients, while others concentrate on offering a specific service such as savings and credit. The latter is often referred to as the minimalist approach, and this type of support in the form of small and particularly microenterprise credit has gained much favour in recent years.

The provision of micro-finance appears to be one form of enterprise development assistance that can benefit the poor, particularly rural women, as well as having the potential to pay for itself. Of course, private moneylenders have demonstrated this for centuries, but micro-finance projects, and related institutions, have been able to offer financial services to the poor in many countries at what appear to be affordable prices, and are still able to cover their own operating and financial costs. Where total sustainability is not immediately achievable, indicators can be put in place to monitor the extent to which operating costs are recovered from income, and improvements in the cost recovery rate can be measured over time.

Some reference has already been made to the implications of this development on evaluation approaches and procedures. It is argued that the emphasis must shift from the measurement of a project's impact on its beneficiaries and its related costs, to assessing the overall sustainability of the institution itself, which it is hoped can carry on delivering services to its clients long after the donor assistance or subsidy has been stopped.

The emphasis on institutional sustainability has led to the development of an incremental ranking system, starting with coverage of operational costs and leading eventually to full cost coverage and the generation of surpluses, even after taking account of loan losses, the cost of funds and providing for the effects of inflation. A number of NGOs throughout the world are working their way up this ladder of sustainability, and towards the eventual goal of being converted into independent financial institutions in their own right. There are various definitions of the different levels of sustainability relating to the degree of the institution's dependence on grants or soft loans to cover their various cost items.   The various "rungs" of this ladder all relate to the sustainability of the institution itself.   They have no direct relationship to the impact of its services on client enterprises or their households.

Bancosol in Bolivia is one organisation which has attained the goal of becoming a financial institution (Mosley, 1993), and other institutions, such as the Grameen Bank in Bangladesh or the Unit Desa programme of the Bank Rakyat Indonesia, have enjoyed banking status for many years. Some of these institutions have already managed to cover all their costs, while others may aim to do so in the near future. The Indonesian case has proved to be highly profitable.

Evaluation Issues for Micro-Finance Schemes

The literature on micro-finance is replete with examples of evaluation studies of institutions which focus on the issues of sustainability or eventual profitability. The original objectives of these institutions were usually limited to providing credit and, when possible, savings services to the owners of microenterprises. However, as Rhyne (1994) points out, these institutions satisfy a wide range of household and community needs, and should be considered as a new kind of financial service institution, rather than only as a form of enterprise assistance. Therefore, it could be argued that their evaluation should not be covered in this book, although a large number of enterprise assistance programmes now concentrate on minimalist financial services.

It must always be recognised, however, that even if these institutions become self-sustaining in the long term, they came into being as a means of making a significant difference to the lives of a specified target group, normally the urban or rural poor. Consequently, the impact that they have on the lives of these people must continue to be evaluated, at the same time as the institution's own performance and operations are being monitored. A profit-seeking commercial business — whether a bank, a trader or a manufacturer — can usually be evaluated exclusively in terms of its profitability, since profits are the owners' objective. The combined effects of market competition and the legal environment should (although they often do not) ensure that customers' decisions about what to buy, where to buy, and whom to buy from are in their own best interests.

The market for financial services, however, is by no means a perfect one, particularly in rural and remote areas, as well as for the poor and disadvantaged clients of the micro-finance institutions. The only competition may be traditional moneylenders whose services are often grossly over-priced for a number of reasons, and who often employ socially destructive techniques for securing repayment, such as bonded labour of various kinds. In situations where the target group is in poverty, and the clients have the burden of repaying principal as well as regular interest payments, there is a very real danger that a micro-finance institution can end up appropriating an inordinately large share of its clients' incomes. It is argued that the resulting revenues for the lending institution are necessary for its sustainability, as well as to pay the large numbers of staff which many micro-finance systems require. But these staff, however well-trained and highly motivated, are usually members of the educated elite. Some financial institutions of this kind may even be regarded as yet another example of the ingenuity with which the rich expropriate the earnings of the poor, consequently perpetuating the cycle of poverty, and negating the original stated objectives of some such programmes.

The literature on this subject generally implies, however, that impact assessment should not focus on the measurement of increases in client incomes or any improvement in their quality of life, with all of the associated problems of collecting data from clients and matched control groups. Such techniques, Rhyne claims, are almost prohibitively expensive for most programmes to use, so that they tend to rely instead on clients' subjective responses. These are frequently based on information arising from memory recall, which is "of little value except for public relations purposes".

Based on experience of several micro-finance schemes in the Philippines, a conceptual framework was formulated by Chua and Llanto (1996) to assess schemes using the five criteria of effectiveness, outreach, efficiency, viability and sustainability of the schemes. Consequently, they have suggested that micro-finance schemes can be assessed in the context of these five criteria.

Evaluation Studies of Micro-Finance Schemes

It is interesting to note that not all small-scale finance schemes appreciate the benefits of impact assessment. The Small Enterprises Finance Company (SEFCO) in Kenya has made no attempts to "undertake a formal impact study ... partly because the institution holds the view that assessing impact especially on clients is a difficult and highly subjective exercise" (SEFCO, 1996). However, from whatever sources of information it has drawn on, SEFCO claims to be able to estimate that 600 of its funded projects will have on average 20 direct employees, giving employment creation figures of about 12,000 jobs which, along with other casual jobs created would give a total of 15,000 jobs. By adopting some systematic measures of impact assessment, perhaps SEFCO would be in a position to move away from its own subjective estimates, and be able to quantify outcomes and impacts objectively.

A 1991 study (Chowdhury and Abed, 1991) of the impact of the Bangladesh Rural Advancement Committee (BRAC) on its clients showed that their quality of life had improved by an average of thirty per cent, measured in terms such as nutrition and possession of household assets, as well as income increases. Similar results were reported on the Grameen Bank's impact on its clients in Bangladesh. A later study of BRAC's clients (Hulme, 1995) showed that the percentage, and of course the absolute increases in incomes of poorer clients, were far smaller than for richer ones and the poorest actually experienced very little change at all. There was also no evidence of the measurement of any other changes or improvements that might have been more important and significant than increases in income.

There is also some evidence that the damaging effects of market saturation are beginning to outweigh the advantages of replacing money-lender loans with institutional micro-credit. Repayments of loan principal and interest may continue, and group pressure can be sustained to ensure that members repay, even if they are worse off than before as a result of their borrowing. The actual impact on the poorest people may turn out to be negative, long before any evaluation of the institution or even an open-ended impact study (such as that recommended by Rhyne) reveals that anything is wrong.

The client profile may also change as management and field staff work towards higher earnings and lower costs by giving preference to larger and longer-term loans for established clients, over small short-term credit for poor people operating at the margin. This upward "client drift" can already be observed in some programmes in Kenya, where donor withdrawal is imminent and the pressure for sustainability is therefore very great. This can be exacerbated by the apparently irrational behaviour of clients who prefer to continue borrowing from the programme at very high rates of interest, rather than taking the feasible and available opportunity of transferring to a commercial bank.

The reasons for this are complex, and relate as much to the attitudes of bankers as to those of the borrowers. The cumulative effect is to allow, and even encourage, the lending agency to neglect its original mission in order to both satisfy existing clients and cover costs.

There is no doubt that the emphasis on institutional sustainability and the reduction and eventual removal of subsidy is correct. This is because problems of poverty and unemployment, which enterprise development projects aim to relieve, are so serious and widespread that they cannot be solved within the life-time of a project. Hospitals are not usually closed down after they have cured some people of some illnesses. Similarly, there is a long-term need for enterprise development institutions to continue providing a range of remedies for a range of clients. As indicated earlier, in a marketing sense the institutions could offer differentiated services to a range of market segments.

The quest for total cost recovery can, nevertheless, lead to a misconception as to the nature of subsidy, particularly when it is applied to the new generation of financial institutions that are emerging from NGOs. Yaron's "subsidy dependence index" (SDI) represents what is perhaps the best attempt to measure the extent to which financial institutions depend on subsidy (Yaron, 1992). It takes account of free equity capital, as well as cheap or interest-free loan funds. However, very few NGOs capitalise their grant finance, particularly at the early stages, and development banks themselves usually treat grants for training and other investments in their institutional development as revenue items rather than as additional sources of capital.

An apparently self-sustaining institution is likely to have been the recipient of development support over a long period, and much of the cost of this development may not be apparent in its balance sheet. The investment in institutional capacity may or may not have yielded value for money for the donors. However, the fact that the institution manages to cover its costs, or even that it has an SDI which is low, zero or negative, is not in itself sufficient evidence that the benefits which its clients are receiving represent a good return on the resources that have been invested in it. Evaluation has to go beyond sustainability and adopt a wider perspective in measuring value for money and impact assessment.

Chapter 7

Outstanding Issues in Evaluation

The various evaluation studies of SED programmes which have been described have their share of methodological weaknesses and may be subject to many different interpretations. They do seem to show, however, that many of the programmes which were evaluated did achieve substantial results, which generally represented value for money for their sponsors.

The cases reported in Chapter 3 also suggest that the standard and rigour of evaluation practice are likely to be higher when local institutions are being evaluated by local staff in less developed countries, than when the programmes are funded by foreign donors (e.g. the CEFE programme), or are implemented in an industrialised country, such as the case in the Cranfield GEP in the United Kingdom.

Client as Customer

If the aim of an SED project is to create a sustainable institution which covers all its costs from interest payments or other client fees, evaluators should perhaps act like market researchers engaged on behalf of any commercial firm. They should gather clients' opinions concerning the services they are receiving from the institution, rather than trying to assess the impact of its services in a more impersonal way. They should also assess key factors such as programme outreach, to ensure that it is reaching the intended target group. They should make use of open-ended research techniques to assess the ways — qualitative as well as quantitative —

in which clients themselves perceive that their lives have been changed as a result of project interventions. Increased self-confidence, empowerment, the improved ability to deal with social situations and unexpected difficulties, such as sickness, the need for a dowry, access to preferred sources of supply, or improved status of women within the family and the community, may be more important to clients than simple increases in income or other limited objectives established by evaluators.

However, the overall emphasis of this form of evaluation is seen to be on "the market test". As with any business, if people voluntarily buy its services at a price that covers the costs, it is generally felt that all is well. This essentially market-led approach to evaluation has much to commend it. In principle it seems consistent that project support interventions which are intended to develop viable enterprises should themselves be judged by standards similar to those which the market imposes on the small businesses. Such projects should practise what they preach.

Project planning, as well as evaluation procedures, can also benefit from adopting marketing techniques. A clearer focus can be placed on client needs by providing a range of differentiated products or services to a variety of market segments. The recently established INASIA organisation — created out of Innovation and Research for Development (IRED) — is looking at ways of developing a typology of target beneficiaries in order to tailor and offer more appropriate services for the respective client segments. In this way enhanced value for money should be assured for donors, implementers and beneficiaries alike by tailoring and targeting services at specific groups.

In certain circumstances the service providers may find it more difficult to deal with "customers" than with people who regard themselves as the objects of charity. We should not lose sight of the fact that continuous customer evaluation based on willingness to pay can be far more effective than anything that can be achieved by periodic studies, however sophisticated the techniques that are used.

This willingness to pay is often suggested as a means of evaluation, whether or not a fee is actually demanded (Harper, 1984b, p.178; Kobb, 1996). Experience has shown that the levels of fees which most small business people are able to pay are unlikely to cover the full costs of training (Sweeting, 1993; Reichert and Herath, 1996a). However, there is much to be said for the imposition of a small charge, in cash or in kind, which may even be almost irrelevant in relation to real costs, but is significant to clients. This acts as an ongoing evaluation device and can prove to be an indicator of the clients' "value for money" assessment of the services they are receiving. It also encourages clients themselves to insist on the maintenance of quality, rather than regarding the service as an act of charity for which they should be grateful.

SED projects can also be concerned with influencing policies and addressing political issues. Governments, and indeed donors, are often in a position where they need to be seen to be doing something about controversial issues such as unemployment. Therefore, the high public visibility of some SED programmes can be far more important to them than any long-term results.

Who Benefits?

The question of "who is to benefit from the programme" raises further issues. Many enterprise development programmes have the explicit objective of assisting particular disadvantaged groups, such as women, youth, the disabled or members of minority or majority racial groups who are felt to have been excluded from the economy. This focus implies that the particular group is, in some sense, more deserving than others, and one obvious way of steering benefits to a chosen group is to add a premium weighting to them in any evaluation.

Distributional weightings are sometimes used in national economic policy analysis, but it has been stated (Devarajan, 1995, p.7) that they are not part of the World Bank's procedures because they are difficult to estimate, subjective and likely to encourage inefficiency. The ODA has also never used such weightings (Wilmshurst, 1995), although they have been considered. At least in the area of small enterprise development, effective targeting should be the preferred method of ensuring that a chosen distributional focus is maintained.

As with many development programmes, small enterprise assistance is often hijacked by less needy groups. The way to prevent this is not to use differential weightings for benefits, but to ensure that the services which are offered are genuinely tailored to the needs of the intended clients, or to the specified market segment. Very small loans, at affordable but higher than market interest rates, which also require regular saving and attendance at group meetings, are only attractive to those who need them. Training, extension and other services should be similarly designed to address the needs of a chosen market, not only to encourage others to exclude themselves, but also to ensure that the services are genuinely appropriate for those whom they are intended to benefit.

Separating Effects

The studies referred to in earlier chapters point to some tentative conclusions about evaluation as such. They demonstrate that it is possible to construct and use control groups, at least for the purpose of one-off evaluation studies, and although the comparative data may itself point in more than one direction, it is worthwhile to make the effort to identify a control group rather than to make no effort to attempt to isolate the effects of the training.

While control groups do allow some comparison between those who participated in a programme and those who do not, they do not provide any information about the effects of various components of the programme, such as behavioural or skills training, or the impact of post-training follow-up, if it is provided. The International Centre for Entrepreneurship and Career Development of Ahmedabad (India) has reported one attempt to disaggregate the effects of the behavioural component from other parts of their Women's Entrepreneurship Development Programme (Harper and Mahajan, 1992). The behavioural component was deliberately omitted from one programme, and those trainees apparently performed significantly worse than others who received the complete package. Management Systems International (McBer and Company/MSI, 1984) also attempted to use control groups to determine the effect of their newly developed competence training when it was being tested in Malawi, Ecuador and India by offering placebo training sessions in book-keeping and so on to control groups, instead of the competence training. Here again, the results are said to have shown that the competence component had a significantly favourable impact on the trainees.

The report of the UN Task Force states that indicators should be "specifically and objectively verifiable measures of change brought about by an activity" (UN ACC Task Force, 1984, p.36). In reality, specificity and objective measurement may be difficult to achieve, but the problem of isolating the effects is even more intractable.

There is a wide range of opinion on whether any attempt should be made to separate the effects of small enterprise development inputs. The USAID 1985 study on "Searching for Benefits" acknowledged some of the difficulties, particularly those relating to control groups, by stating that "control groups are not an available choice", because "firms only co-operate with those who demand sensitive information if it is a precondition for a loan or technical assistance. Except under unusual circumstances, entrepreneurs will not agree to serve as a control group" (Kilby and Z'mura, 1985, p.9). The subsequent 1989 study (Boomgard, 1989, p.29), which generally takes a less dogmatic view on many issues, concluded that the two critical issues of isolating the effects and measuring the sustainability of the benefits remain unresolved.

There is no question that the identification and use of control groups present many problems even in pilot studies, such as the cost-benefit analysis of an early entrepreneurship development programme in Nepal to which reference has already been made. The sheer act of applying for a loan or for a training place is in itself an act of self-selection by the entrepreneur. Therefore, the only way to obtain a similar group for control purposes is by the random rejection of people who would otherwise have been selected. This is clearly an unjust approach for those who are rejected, as well as being quite rightly unpopular with project staff who want to be shown to achieve the best results. Furthermore, the process of identifying such a group can be quite impractical in many real-life situations.

If the development input has been in the form of training or consultancy services that enables business owners to maintain reasonable records of their financial results, it may be impossible to obtain comparable data from a control group who have not been trained in these techniques. The very act of obtaining data from the control group may also affect them positively or negatively (UN ACC Task Force, 1984, p.45), by what is sometimes referred to as the "goldfish bowl effect". On the whole, the weight of published opinion (Freeman, 1979, p.33) is against the use of control groups, for a whole range of reasons.

Alternative approaches to the isolation of effects may be easier to use but seem generally less valid. One World Bank project in Indonesia (Levitzky, 1986, p.303) compared the performance of a sample of enterprises that received loans in 1979 with data obtained for the same period from another group which received loans in 1982. This was done in order to obtain comparable data on those "with loans" and those "without loans" for the three-year period. This of course begs the question of how similar the 1982 recipients were to the 1979 ones and, if they were similar, why they had not been the recipients of loans at the same time. In this, as in many other cases, evaluators relied on clients' recall of their earlier performance, as well as in their views of how they would have performed without the services they had received (Bolnick and Nelson, 1990, p.300).

Haggblade (1992), in his "general model" for evaluation, suggests that as an alternative to control groups, clients' performance can be compared with "standard indicators of economic activity", such as the level of sales in the local market. This can have the added weakness of depending on approximations of local market conditions, but it may be sufficient if the intention is to find out whether an assistance programme has had any significant effect on clients at all, rather than to attempt to quantify it precisely. A similar informal ex-post approach was used in Kenya (Harper, 1974) where the percentage improvement in client performance was calculated and found to be clearly far greater than even the most optimistic assessments of economic growth that would have been produced for the markets where the target group of entrepreneurs operated. This was taken as a general indicator that the particular experiment had been useful. It would not, however, have been sufficient for the precise calculation of the rate of return on investment or to analyse the costs and benefits in detail.

These and similar alternative approaches clearly have their shortcomings, but in spite of the numerous difficulties there are several cases when control groups have been used with success, and where evaluation has been a great deal more informative as a result. The various studies of the EDPs in India which were described in Chapter 3, the study of BRAC and Grameen Bank clients in Bangladesh (Chowdhury and Abed, 1991), and the comparison of the cost-effectiveness of EDPs and small business consultancy in Nepal (Harper, 1984b, p.184-186) all demonstrate that when it is necessary to have information about the actual effects of a programme, it can be obtained. Such information is by no means always necessary, and the data are likely to suffer from the same weaknesses as the findings of any social science investigation. However, the very real difficulties of using control groups — or other rigorous approaches — should not be an excuse for abandoning them completely. Once an evaluation procedure has been adopted, even one which is less than perfect, comparisons and trends can be identified and extracted from periodic reports produced under such an evaluation framework. This information will prove to be invaluable for monitoring and management purposes, both for the implementing agency as well as the donor.

Whose Time-frame?

It may be worthwhile to reflect on some of the authors' experiences where donor time-frames appeared unrealistic in the light of the prevailing needs. From 1988 to 1991, UNDP had funded a project to promote self-employment and youth enterprise in Zambia. The project was designed at a time when individual enterprise endeavour and entrepreneurial initiative were frowned upon by the Zambian government which operated a command economy. It was also acknowledged that enterprise programmes targeted specifically at young people can be problematic as many lack the maturity, responsibility, experience and skills for small enterprise development. However, by the end of the three-year period, considerable interest had been generated in the whole idea of self-employment and small enterprise development, among both policy-makers and the youth themselves. In addition, local role models had been created and a national association of youth entrepreneurs had been established. Prospects for sustainability had been improved through a number of institution-building initiatives with government and non-governmental organisations. In short, the groundwork had been laid and the seeds of youth enterprise had been sown. Furthermore, the political climate had altered dramatically to become more supportive of individual enterprise initiatives and the government had embarked on programmes in support of market liberalisation and privatisation. Much could have been gained from further donor investment in such a project. However, the donor had other priorities and the youth enterprise movement in the country was not only frustrated by the sudden switching off of donor assistance, but also by having their expectations raised during the project's life. Specific activities, such as the project's Loan Guarantee Fund, were discontinued in mid-stream and, armed with that knowledge, repayments by the young entrepreneurs ceased almost overnight. After several years, it was left to other donors, such as the Irish Government's technical assistance programme (Irish Aid), to revitalise and develop some of the initiatives implemented by the former ILO-UNDP project in Zambia.

In another illustration, the cease-fire called by the Irish Republican Army and other paramilitary groups in Northern Ireland during 1995-96 brought with it a large amount of goodwill and many offers of financial support from the international community. The European Union, the US Government and the International Fund for Ireland were willing to provide funding for the process of peace, reconciliation and reconstruction both in Northern Ireland and the border areas of the Republic of Ireland.

For many years, Northern Ireland has had a very high level of community and local economic development activity, with due attention being given to establishing appropriate processes aimed at bringing about tangible improvements in local communities and local economies in the long-term. Many community activists expressed their concerns about the sudden massive injection of donor funds which were to be introduced over a short and finite time-frame. There was much donor talk of substantial and tangible "flagship projects" and the need for high visibility to be given to their funded activities. Yet it appeared that little consideration was being shown for the well-established processes of local economic development and empowerment of people at the community level. Donors wanted to see a quick return on their investment within their specified time frames, seemingly regardless of the longer-term implications and impact which such an investment would have on the local communities and on existing community structures and processes.

Levels of Evaluation

Evaluation can be carried out at different levels. Gibb recommends that entrepreneurship development programmes should be evaluated at the following levels (Gibb, 1991):

i) *The reaction evaluation level* — noting participants' immediate reaction to the programme in terms of its relevance; amount learned; appropriate style of teaching, and views of its usefulness in practice.

ii) *The learning of the participants* — in particular what knowledge and skills have been acquired. This can often be measured by "before" and "after" testing.

iii) *Behaviour changes of clients* — seeking to measure whether the programme has led to changes in behaviour through the application of new knowledge, skills and attitudes.

iv) *Organisational changes* — seeking to measure what kind of organisational impact has been made resulting from any behaviour change, e.g. in the case of a business start-up programme, how many businesses have actually been started.

v) *The ultimate results of the training* — in terms of the impact upon turnover, profit and employment, and of the inter-relationship of training with other factors impacting upon these ultimate criteria.

Gibb also suggests that "such evaluations will need to include summative statements (measuring outputs resulting from) as well as formative statements (measuring the efficiency and effectiveness of) the inputs and process of training" (Gibb, 1991).

In acknowledging the difficulties associated with attempting to isolate the impact of training on small firm performance, Cushion (1995) proposes an alternative innovative framework for measuring success, based on feedback from small business owner managers. The framework, which has been developed though the Norfolk

Small Business Initiative (NSBI) in the United Kingdom, uses three areas of focus, not dissimilar to the levels suggested by Gibb.

• The product focus seeks to address questions about the quality of the training product.

• The customer focus examines the reaction of the customers (the small business owners) to the training product and the impact it has on their business.

• The organisational focus considers the best way in which to organise training delivery.

Cushion suggests that the complexity of the small business training system and the nature of delivery requires "a raft of diverse qualitative and quantitative approaches" to measure success. His summary of the evaluation of NSBI's own programmes states that by July 1995 over 300 businesses had been trained and 95 per cent of participants said they would definitely recommend the course to others, while 67 per cent gave it the highest possible rating. The NSBI experience stresses the value of having customer-driven training programmes, as well as participatory evaluation procedures.

The monitoring and evaluation system developed by the UNDP/ILO Entrepreneurship Education Project in Kenya is another good example of evaluation being carried out at different levels. It covered the policy, institutional and enterprise levels, and adopted both short-run and long-run time-frames in its evaluation procedures. Information for the evaluations was gathered using a variety of techniques, including studies, reports, field visits, interviews, observations and examinations (Mburugu and Thiongo, 1996).

Success indicators at the three designated levels were as shown in Box 7.1. The framework illustrated in Box 7.1 was used to determine the programme's performance, with quantifiable measures of impact assessment designed for each of the three levels.

Box 7.1: Success indicators	
Short run	**Long run**
Policy Level	
• Number of Policies put in place. • Numbers and calibre of government officials supporting the programme.	• Mechanism for reviewing, improving and sustaining policies related to the programme. • Degree of effectiveness in policy implementation. • Establishment of permanent government officials in positions to guide the programme.
Institutional Level	
• Number of institutional administrators and trainers oriented and supportive of the programme. • Number of institutions offering the programme. • Number of Small Business Centres started to provide linkage with business/industrial communities. • Number of activities conducted by Centres. • Amount and quality of training materials being developed and used.	• System for developing administrators and trainers. • System for following-up ex-graduates. • Quality of start-up programmes offered by Centres. • Contribution of private sector to the programme. • Mechanism for continued review and development of materials.
Enterprise level (Entrepreneur level)	
• Number of potential entrepreneurs reached. • Number of viable business plans produced. • Number of enterprises started.	• Positive attitudes towards entrepreneurship and self-employment.

A Hierarchy of Evaluation Measures

It is possible to construct a hierarchy of evaluation measures for any small enterprise development activity. Box 7.2 summarises a hierarchy which is appropriate for EDPs, and demonstrates that the easiest and quickest measures may also be the least realistic, in that they tend to measure inputs and not outputs. In Box 7.2 these include most of the items listed from 1 to 6, although the number of participants trained may also be regarded as an output of the training. Items 7 to 15 provide measures of outputs, and items 16 and 17 provide an impression and statement of the sustainability of the training programmes. Box 7.2 also shows the possible cost-benefit assessment which may be done in respect of some of the output measures. The quality of all the output measures, and thus of any cost-benefit assessment, can also be improved by the use of control groups and by drawing comparisons with the performance of non-participants.

It is most useful to construct such a hierarchy when a project or programme is at the design stage and when evaluation procedures are being considered. At this point the decision should be taken on the measures to be used, whether they should be related to the costs incurred, and whether an attempt should be made to isolate the effects of the intervention.

Training in Evaluation Techniques

Training can be provided in evaluation techniques and some efforts have been made to do so in Ireland by FAS, the national training and employment agency. As an integral part of its Community Enterprise Programme FAS has introduced various Open Learning Units to upgrade the skills of its community-based workers and supervisors through a series of self-study guides (FAS, undated). On the theme of Community Employment, there is a specialised Open Learning Unit on Evaluation in which the purpose and process of evaluation are clearly defined. Suggested principles for defining an evaluation exercise include:

Box 7.2: A hierarchy of measures for evaluating EDPs

	Measure	Cost-Benefit
1.	Funding obtained	N/A
2.	Trainers recruited	N/A
3.	Trainers trained	N/A
4.	Participants recruited	N/A
5.	Participants trained	Cost per trainee
6.	Participant evaluations	N/A
7.	Business plans completed	N/A
8.	Loans sanctioned	N/A
9.	Businesses started	Cost per business
10.	Numbers employed	Cost per job
11.	Capital invested	Cost:capital ratio
12.	Sales made	Sales:cost RoI
13.	Value added	Value added:cost RoI
14.	Profits earned	Profit:cost RoI
15.	Taxes paid	Taxes: cost RoI
16.	Willingness to pay	N/A
17.	Full cost fees paid	Profitability of institution

Notes on Box 7.2

Item 9: The total cost of training divided by the number of businesses started — the lower the better.

Item 10: The total cost of training divided by the number of full-time equivalent jobs created — the lower the better.

Item 11: The total cost of training as a proportion (ratio) of the capital invested in the enterprise — the higher the capital invested the better.

Item 12: Sales made by the enterprise as a percentage of the cost of training — in addition this provides a rough indicator of the Return on the Investment (RoI) in training.

Item 13: The Value Added as a percentage of the cost of training — this is a more conservative indicator of the Return on the Investment in training (RoI).

Item 14: Profits made as a percentage of the cost of training — a further measure of RoI.

Item 15: Taxes paid as a percentage of the costs of training — this can be an important indicator of the RoI on the government's investment in an EDP training initiative.

Item 17: This is an important measure of the extent to which the institution is recovering, fully covering or indeed making a profit on its EDP training activities, thus demonstrating the potential for financial independence from donor assistance and the long-term commercial viability of the training programmes.

- Evaluation should have a purpose: you should be clear about what you want the evaluation to achieve.
- Evaluation should be based on stated assumptions and standards: you should clarify the assumptions and standards on which you are evaluating.
- Evaluation should be co-operative: you should involve all of those people who have been involved in the subject being evaluated.
- Evaluation should be continuous: evaluation should not be left until the very end of a project — you should start evaluating from the beginning of a project and continue reviewing it throughout.

Such comprehensive approaches aimed at training staff in evaluation techniques are to be applauded as they can contribute over time to improving the overall quality of evaluations carried out.

Life Expectancy of Enterprises

It has to be recognised that a large proportion of small enterprises go out of existence, either because they fail or because their owners find preferable ways of earning a living. Others survive and a smaller number expand and eventually become medium or even large businesses. Research into the growth of metal-working businesses in Zimbabwe (Neshamba, 1995) shows how some informal enterprises do evolve into significant formal employers, and a loan or training programme may well be the stimulus that enables some of the potential "winners" to expand. In other cases the effect of the assistance programme may be to prevent the business from "falling sick" or dying, but this too is an equally real benefit which merits measurement. The jobs which are saved by assisting such ailing enterprises are also worthy of measurement.

The literature is largely silent on how the difficulty of forecasting the expected life of an enterprise can be overcome, but it is often possible to make an approximate assessment of the average life of a business of the type that is being assisted. It is conservative to assume that clients' businesses will last no longer than the average of all businesses, and this assumption may therefore be acceptable.

The same issue arises in the context of investment in institutional capacity. Whatever measurement was used to assess the benefits, the return on the funds spent on the original USAID assistance which played such an important part in the evolution of the highly successful BRI Unit Desa Banking system in Indonesia, would obviously be enormous. It is a fact, however, that institutions themselves are no more immortal than the businesses they assist. Accountants are always supposed to be conservative in their valuation of inventory and other items that are likely to affect the calculation of profits; evaluators should be no less cautious in their calculations.

Calculating Costs and Benefits

When data have been obtained covering past performance, or relating to estimates made for the future, it can still be argued that these figures will have to be modified to take account of when and by whom the costs were incurred or the benefits gained. Consideration must also be given to the duration for which the costs and benefits arising from the project intervention may be expected to continue.

Discounting, which takes account of what is referred to as the "time value of money", that is the fact that it is better to have one dollar today than one dollar five years from today, is typically used in project appraisal rather than for project evaluation purposes. However, it is recognised that almost every evaluation is concerned with costs and benefits that have taken place at different times in the past, and particularly with benefits which are estimated to arise at various times in the future.

It seems reasonable to discount future amounts to take account of the time value of money. Most people would agree that benefits which are earned or costs which are incurred today are in some way worth more than those which may occur five years from now, whether or not they accept the notion of the "opportunity cost" of funds - meaning that the same funds could have been put to other alternative uses during the intervening period. This is particularly appropriate in conditions of high inflation that characterise so many less developed economies, but inflation is by its nature unpredictable. It can be convincingly argued (Sell, 1992) that there is no point in attempting to adjust project appraisal or evaluation data for inflation, even in countries with high inflation rates, because of the unreliability of the data and other methodological difficulties. There are also a number of serious conceptual problems that have thrown the whole technique of discounting into some disrepute, particularly when it is applied to social as opposed to pure "business" projects.

If future benefits are discounted even at a very low rate, any investment in enterprise education for school children will become far less attractive than projects with a more rapid return. This may in part explain the preference of many agencies such as USAID (Kilby and Z'mura, 1985, p.119) for minimalist credit, which yields rather rapid returns in client incomes, as opposed to human capital development activities such as training or extension services, which have a slower, longer and perhaps less tangible payback.

At a practical level, the choice of a discount rate is as much a political as an economic issue, and because there is no "right" rate there is a tendency to choose a rate that presents a favourable picture. This clearly shows that the technique itself is open to question.

The 1985 USAID study (Kilby and Z'mura, 1985) however, uses discounting to compare five different small enterprise development projects, and it is difficult to see how this could have been done in any other way. The present value of the benefits in all five projects exceeds the costs, by margins ranging from 1.019 to 8.172 times, and the figures also take account of the likely effect of inflation on the results. This comparison demonstrates the importance of ensuring a rapid start to project operations, as well as the advantages of working with an existing organisation as opposed to developing a new one. These are surely points with which nobody would quarrel.

In a general sense, discounting future flows of funds implies that there is a lower valuation put on benefits to future generations than to one's own, and this has been shown to be quite unacceptable and even absurd when applied to projects with important environmental implications, such as for small enterprise projects affecting natural resource depletion, forestry, or hazardous waste disposal (Price, 1995). The same arguments clearly apply to poverty-alleviation programmes having a long-term perspective, and although no satisfactory alternative system has been developed (Livingstone and Tribe, 1995), it is suggested that discounting should only be applied in exceptional cases, and any conclusions based on discounted data should be treated with caution.

The issue of whether future benefits should be adjusted to take account of their timing is a difficult one, but it is more important — and more difficult — to assess the duration for which such benefits will continue to flow, and at what level. Small enterprise development necessarily involves investing known amounts today in the hope of unknown but hoped for benefits tomorrow. Of course the sustainability of these benefits is as important a factor as their magnitude, as the number of enterprises which achieve them (Boomgard, 1989, p.24).

As has already been pointed out, most evaluation takes place during the period of direct subsidy or support, or immediately thereafter. If the only benefits to be taken into account are those already achieved during the project's life, the results of the evaluation will end up being dependent on the date of the evaluation and not on the merits of the development intervention. The logical framework that is now being used by many donor agencies provides a convenient column for "assumptions" (European Union, 1993; Famiyeh, 1995) in which statements can be made about many aspects of project implementation, such as the expected time-frame for benefits and the likely level of government support. However, these statements do not go far enough, they can be conveniently vague and they fall short of solving the problem.

It is often claimed that it is not practical to obtain financial data from small-scale entrepreneurs in order to quantify and evaluate their performance. The studies carried out by Management Systems International (MSI) appear to contradict this, although the entrepreneurs in question usually ran more formal enterprises, thus making financial record-keeping an easier task than for most micro-enterprise development programmes. In addition, the very nature of the training programmes was such as to enable the trainees to produce financial data which helped in evaluation. However, there have been occasions where some business trainers could be accused of adopting teaching techniques that are of more benefit to the training institution in its efforts to justify its own work, than to the business owners themselves as the trainees. In this context, a balance should be maintained between the benefits accruing to the trainee entrepreneurs, and the institution's own reporting and monitoring mechanisms.

If there is to be any attempt to assess the efficiency of SED, or to calculate the return on the sums that are invested in it, it is obviously necessary to know the costs as well as the benefits. Although many development organisations, and in particular NGOs, have little idea of their total costs, and still less knowledge of the costs of particular activities, it is undoubtedly easier to calculate the costs of making a loan or running a training programme than it is to assess the benefits that may result from them.

There are, nevertheless, a number of important difficulties that are likely to lead to the serious understatement of costs, and thus to unrealistic overestimates of efficiency. If clients are paying the full cost of a service they should be expected to take into account their own costs, which will include the cost of the transaction, as well as the actual payment they make for the service. Indeed this explains why many poor people still prefer to borrow money from moneylenders at apparently extortionate interest rates, rather than to benefit from NGOs' micro-credit schemes. When the clients' own transaction costs, such as inconvenience, lost time and transport costs are included, borrowing from a local moneylender can actually be cheaper than many subsidised credit schemes.

Good business practice requires that the total cost to the customer is minimised in relation to the benefit received, and small enterprise assistance — whether it is sold for its full cost, subsidised or free — must still be well marketed in accordance with good business practice. There is evidence (Harper A, 1995, p.8) that clients of some micro-finance programmes are becoming over-burdened with the transaction costs that have effectively been passed on to them by the lending system which they have chosen.

The low attendance at many small enterprise training programmes can be explained, not simply by the lack of relevance of some of what is taught, but also by the inconvenience of the timing, the inappropriateness of the location, and the failure of project staff to appreciate that business people lose money when they are absent from their enterprises. There is an opportunity cost to the entrepreneur. The total client costs must be assessed and included in the cost-benefit equation unless and until the fees that are charged cover all the costs of provision, and until competitive providers exist. At this point the clients themselves can be assumed to be making the necessary market assessment on behalf of themselves and looking after their own best business interests.

Foreign or donor overhead costs are another category that is often omitted or understated in project evaluation. This can arise because it is anticipated that international or other donor assistance will only be necessary for the initial pilot phase. Thereafter, it is hoped, the methodology will be successfully replicated and only recurring local costs will be involved.

Another item that is often underestimated or omitted is the cost of complementary (and sometimes complimentary) inputs which clients may have received from other agencies. As has already been pointed out above, in the Indian evaluations the EDP trainees were not only trained, but were also assisted to find their way through the maze of support institutions in order to gain access to other services. One of these may have been subsidised credit or grants, but they may also have included other training, or access to premises or utilities, all of which were and generally still are heavily subsidised in India.

It would be very difficult to assess the total cost of all the services received by the enterprises that had been established by the EDP trainees, as well as to compare this with similar data for a control group. However, if a wide range of subsidised services is available for small businesses, it is important to ensure that every project does not take all of the credit for the entire extent of every success, and an estimate of the costs of pertinent services should be included in any cost-benefit assessment. This is particularly the case when those businesses which have access to one service are for that very reason also likely to be able to access others.

There is a strong case for using shadow prices to adjust the costs of inputs such as foreign exchange, loan capital or wages because of distortions arising from government subsidies and other mechanisms, or because of the low opportunity cost of under-used resources. This has obviously become less of an issue in recent years than it used to be (Devarajan, 1995), as governments have gradually been removing the controls which led to such distortions. However, it can be argued that if enterprise profits are being used as a critical indicator of project benefits, the cost of wages for people who would otherwise be under-employed should be discounted. It might also be argued that some local project costs should be reduced when assessing their economic contribution, because "project" wages and salaries are often well above the market rates for the people who are hired, and even those market rates may be well above the opportunity cost to the economy of unskilled employees.

In spite of the massive weight of evidence as to the damaging effects of cheap credit, heavily subsidised loans are still made available to small enterprises in India and a few other countries. It might have been reasonable to take account of this particular distortion when assessing the increased profits achieved by trainees in the evaluations of Indian EDPs referred to earlier, since privileged access to such funds is an important component in some of these programmes.

However, shadow pricing is probably a technique which should not be seriously considered when evaluating small enterprise development. Such techniques, like discounting future cash flows, may divert attention from the management of programmes to a narrower debate over the choice of percentages. Comparability over time or between programmes is in any case more important than the absolute figures.

Both Oxfam (Rubin, 1995, p.30) and the World Bank (Levitzky, 1986, p.301) criticise cost-benefit analysis. They suggest that its standards tend to be externally imposed, it is too focussed on results rather than processes, and it misses out on identifying unforeseen consequences, whether favourable or otherwise. The 1989 USAID evaluation study (Boomgard, 1989, p.30) accepts that "the ratio of present value of benefits to costs provides the ideal standardised measure of programme performance", but concludes nevertheless that the cost per beneficiary and per dollar lent are more practical indicators, in spite of their admitted weaknesses.

The examples given in earlier chapters, however, demonstrate that the practical difficulties can be overcome, even on a modest budget. There is also a substantial body of opinion in favour of the use of quantitative techniques to relate costs to benefits. The Kenya Industrial Estates (KIE) Informal Sector Programme is a well-regarded integrated project which offers training as well as credit. Its costs are regularly compared with the benefits as part of its planned progress towards sustainability (Eigen, 1992). Haggblade (1992) states categorically that "benefit-cost ratios less than one mean projects should be discontinued", and that it is safe to assume that qualitative benefits will follow from good quantitative results.

A number of authorities in small enterprise development and other fields caution against losing the rigour of cost-benefit analysis because of the emphasis on qualitative measures. "Hard methods for soft policies", is a useful phrase which has been used in the context of environmental impact evaluation (Angelsen and Sumaila, 1995). The ODA (Wilmshurst, 1995) also warns that we should not discard the fundamental principle of comparing costs with benefits.

Social cost-benefit analysis is used as an evaluation technique in many more sensitive fields than SED, such as family planning, health services and education (Freeman, 1979, p.158). In some aspects the ultimate objectives of small enterprise development may be similar to these social projects, but it is the means that are basically different, using the economics of business and involving matters such as revenues, expenses and profits. As the later USAID study concludes (Boomgard, 1989, p.69), "qualitative and quantitative measures... must co-exist in the evaluation process."

The foregoing pages have suggested not only that benefits should be assessed and that costs should be known, but that the two should be compared in order to have some idea of the value for money, cost-benefit ratio or return on investment that has been achieved. This view is by no means universally accepted. Box 7.3 summarises some of the quantitative results that have been reported and which attempt to compare costs with benefits.

Box 7.3: Summary of benefit-cost data in dollars

Cost per job (CDI divided by no. of jobs created): [CDI being total Cost of Development Intervention]
- $ 25 (training, India)
- $ 150 (training, India)
- $ 60 (training, India)
- $ 5,500 (training, UK)
- $ 4,657 (loans, worldwide)
- $ 42 (NGO) and $ 125 (university) (training, Indonesia)
- $ 470 (training, local costs, Nepal)

Ratio of capital raised by entrepreneurs to CDI
- 20.0:1 (India)
- 27.5:1 (India)
- 3.0:1 (UK)

Cost of development support per business created
- $ 500 (India)
- $ 116 (NGO) and $ 218 (university) (training: Indonesia)

Return on CDI estimates
(a) Wages earned as percentage of CDI:
- • 140% and 79% (India)
- • 90% (Cambodia)

(b) Increase in enterprise profits as %age of CDI:
- • 35% (India)
- • 27% (India)

(c) Value added as percentage of CDI:
- • 300% on local costs,
- • 13% on total costs (Nepal)

(d) Taxes to be paid as percentage of CDI:
- 12% (UK)

Source: The above data derived from:
Acharya, 1990; Awasthi and Sebastian, 1992; Brown, 1995; CED, 1990; Harper, 1984; Harper and Mahajan, 1991; ILO, 1993, 1994; McClelland, 1971; World Bank, 1990

The Jury is Still Out on Small Enterprise Development

In the article "Management Training and Small Firm Performance: Why is the Link So Weak?" Westhead and Storey raise fundamental questions about the impact of small business training based on experiences from many countries. Apart from presenting a critique of various SED evaluation studies, the authors recognise the many pitfalls facing evaluators. Difficulties in isolating effects, as well as the distorting impact of external factors on internal performance, are among the issues highlighted. In summary, they point to a "huge growth in the 'training industry', much of it supported by the public purse." They also indicate that small enterprises which have participated in management training schemes have derived some benefit from participation, most notably in their enhanced level of confidence. However, "careful empirical research has failed to link the provision of management training in the small firm with enhanced performance in the recipient firm" (Westhead and Storey, 1996). If anything, the authors' conclusion throws out a challenge for SED practitioners and evaluators alike. Can the impact of SED support programmes (including training) be improved and quantified, and what are the most appropriate ways of evaluating such support interventions?

Chapter 8

The Mechanics of Evaluation

The examples mentioned in the foregoing chapters have illustrated a variety of approaches to the evaluation of a range of small enterprise development programmes. It is also worth remembering that evaluation itself can have many different purposes. It is relatively simple to suggest a methodology for the traditional mid-term or end-of-project evaluations that are associated with development projects lasting no more than three years or so. These evaluations are intended mainly to facilitate decisions about continuation, modification or termination, and are generally carried out by external evaluators selected by the donors.

As the examples in the earlier chapters have shown, this rather static approach to evaluation is becoming increasingly irrelevant, as projects give way to institutions, and the important needs of clients and the roles of project staff are being more widely recognised. The distinction between monitoring the ongoing performance and evaluating the results becomes blurred when evaluation is seen as a routine management tool, rather than as an externally-driven method of judgement.

It is still necessary, however, for all the stakeholders in an activity, such as the clients, employees, managers and sponsors, to know whether it is achieving the objectives that were set for it. As NGOs become more professional and less distinct from commercial contractors, it is vital that donors should not lose sight of the need to ensure that they, as well as the clients, are getting value from the increasing sums of money being spent on development activities implemented by the NGOs. The pressure to involve clients in a participatory evaluation process can lead to the abandonment of any quantifiable or measurable objectives, so that there is a danger that the projects lose all sense of direction or ownership.

As with enterprise development itself, the evaluation process should have a clear set of objectives. The "by whom?", "when?" and "what?" types of questions cannot be answered until we know "for whom?", and "why?" (Rubin, 1995, p.30). If possible, evaluation should be an integral part of the development process and it should be built into the project design ab initio. It should also be a form of education and an important learning experience for all the parties involved (Marsden and Oakley, 1990, p.98). On a more direct level, an evaluation may also be required as the basis for assessing a contractor's payments, in cases where projects have been awarded on a performance basis (Gray, 1995). Also, the main purpose of the evaluation may be to discover whether the service in question needs to be subsidised, or whether it should be part of the public sector provision (Devarajan, 1995). Evaluation must never become a routine or ritual performance, merely to be carried out at a certain time because "that is how things have been done in the past". It must be subject to the same process of justification as the project itself.

There are a number of key decisions that still have to be made in the context of every evaluation situation, regarding who is to be responsible for obtaining whatever information is needed, when it should be obtained, and what exactly the information should be. The following sections briefly address these issues.

Who Should Evaluate?

In the literature on this subject, opinions as to who should evaluate enterprise development activities differ, not only because of the wide range of activities that have to be evaluated, but also depending on the individual perspective of the writer.

The Oxfam approach (Marsden and Oakley, 1990, p.34; Rubin, 1995, p.20) typifies the NGO "bottom-up" view. The dynamics of many evaluation activities all too often involve implementers of a project who want it to appear successful, as much as donors who are suspicious and are looking for faults. As a result, the interests of the clients as the target group are often forgotten. Traditional approaches to evaluation are criticised for being too scientific, too standardised and too dominated by project management and outside evaluators. Aaker and Shumaker (1994, p.9) stress that evaluation should be a joint undertaking by the clients, local project staff, managers and the donors.

A 1984 United Nations document (UN ACC Task Force, 1984, p.51) makes the point that evaluation is an important part of the empowerment process and that if the people who are intended to benefit from an activity are not centrally involved in its evaluation, this necessarily implies that they are not considered competent by the donor or implementing agency. Furthermore, it is a clear statement that they have not been sufficiently empowered as a result of the project's activities.

There are good practical reasons for clients to play a larger role in evaluation, beyond the principles of participation and empowerment or the market research view put forward by the proponents of institutional sustainability (Feuerstein, 1986). External evaluators are expensive, and the time necessary to brief them and guide them through the project may be even more costly. Although it is important not to place excessive demands on the clients themselves, they are often in a position to provide reliable data more economically than any outsider.

Bolnick and Nelson (1990) for instance refer to the effects of rapid staff turnover and lack of experience on the evaluation of the KIK/KMPK programme in Indonesia. The staff of the donor and of the implementing agency had little opportunity to take ownership of the evaluation findings because they were usually transferred before any conclusive evaluation of their work could be undertaken or before findings could be acted upon. These officials also needed special training in evaluation methods that were probably only applied once in their stay with the programme. In these circumstances, it obviously became more effective and efficient to devolve as much as possible of the evaluation function to the clients themselves.

It is easy to preach client participation, but there are also practical reasons for involving external advisers. In its Guidelines paper, the ILO recommends that evaluation reports should have a limited circulation, and as a consequence the documents often have the word "restricted" stamped on them, thus implying that the results are not to be shared with everyone (ILO undated). Earlier studies from the OECD (Imboden, 1978, p.119, Freeman, 1979, p.47), which presumably represent a donor viewpoint, state that evaluation should be done by outsiders and that project planners, who are presumably outsiders, should also be involved in the evaluation process.

This may represent an out-dated "top-down" view of development itself, but a 1995 paper (Jayasundere, 1995, p.23) stated that impact evaluation must be done by an outsider. A recent address by a senior official of the ODA (Wilmshurst, 1995) referred to the growing need for a range of specialists in evaluation, and Haggblade (1992) also suggested that an outsider should be in a position to obtain objective client data, thereby avoiding the tendency for clients to flatter or otherwise ingratiate themselves with project staff.

In the evaluation of CEFE projects the project manager can nominate two of the three evaluators to make up an evaluation team. For most UNDP projects, including those carried out by ILO, the evaluation team is comprised of a donor nominee (representing UNDP), a nominee of the executing agency (e.g. ILO), and a representative of the host implementing agency. However, even these procedures are subject to human error which can ultimately be reflected in the quality of the evaluation. In 1991 one of the authors was nominated to participate in the evaluation of an ILO-UNDP project in Zambia which was managed by the other author. However, due to a mispronunciation or spelling error, the invitation went to a Dutch national of a rather similar name - but who was not a small enterprise specialist - and the evaluation suffered accordingly.

Although many authorities state categorically that a specified group should carry out evaluations, they are usually referring to different levels of evaluation. USAID (Goldmark and Rosengard, 1987) identify three different levels for evaluation as clients, institutions and policy. In so doing, they recognise that one very important result of small enterprise development projects can be changes in the policy environment that indirectly affect all small enterprises, and not only the impact on the very few which benefited from a particular demonstration project.

The OECD (Imboden, 1978, p.129) uses the terms "process evaluation", "implementation evaluation" and "impact evaluation" to make a similar point. As is always the case, there are no hard and fast rules, but the clear statement made by PACT (Buzzard and Edgcomb, 1987) that one should "always collect information as part of routine activities if you can" is a useful general principle. Other levels of evaluation have been referred to in the Chapter 7.

It is obvious that an external evaluator ceases to be an outsider if she or he is involved in a continuous evaluation process. Therefore the choice of who should evaluate is inevitably closely related to when the evaluation takes place. Here again there is a multiplicity of views on the timing of an evaluation. It is worth repeating, however, that the evaluation process will have clearer objectives and direction where the evaluation criteria are built into the design of the project.

When Should Evaluation Take Place?

As has already been pointed out, every form of small enterprise development activity is likely to have a hierarchy of objectives, ranging from immediate and easily measurable inputs, such as the submission of a project proposal or hiring of staff, to long-term outputs which can be difficult to measure accurately, such as improved quality of life (Harper, 1984b, p.173). It is obviously not sufficient to evaluate training or a credit operation only on the short-term outputs such as numbers trained or loans disbursed. However, these indicators have a useful role to play when measuring progress at the early stages.

Oxfam (Rubin 1995, p.33) suggest that some form of evaluation should be undertaken before an activity starts, at an early stage, at mid-term, at the end, and some time thereafter. It is also pointed out that seasonal factors and staff and client workload, must also be taken into account when timing an evaluation exercise. Such recommendations are easier to make than to follow, as the evaluation process itself can be very time consuming and resource demanding.

While it is probably true that ultimate project objectives are often unlikely to be achieved in less than three to five years, it does seem unrealistic to suggest that ex-post evaluations should be carried out "a number of years after completion" (European Union, 1993, p.60), 3–5 five years after completion (Samson, 1996), five years after the end of project (Haggblade, 1992), or even after ten or twenty years (UN ACC Task Force, 1984, p.46). ACCION recommend more reasonable intervals of six and eighteen months after the start of an activity (ACCION/Calmeadow, 1988), but both the World Bank (Devarajan, 1995) and USAID (Boomgard, 1989, p.31) make the point that a donor's last disbursements are likely to be made well before the main benefits can be expected to have revealed themselves. In the commercial world, the projected results from an investment are estimated over a span of several years, such as in business feasibility studies or forecasting the long-term impact and carry-over effect of expenditure on an activity such as an advertising campaign. So too in the case of development projects, efforts should be made to measure the residual impact of an activity over a period beyond the time-constrained life of the project itself.

Businesses, which have the objective of making profits, tend to monitor their activities on a continuous basis. They are obliged to produce audited annual accounts, often more to satisfy shareholders and the law than to evaluate their own operations. However, they have their own management information systems that are designed to enable management to identify and respond almost immediately to opportunities and problems on a continuous basis, and certainly not to await the obligatory periodic evaluation of an audit. There are many enterprise support institutions and agencies which aim at similar standards. The Grameen Bank (Bangladesh) circulates a summary of current data on loan disbursements and repayments on a monthly basis to a world-wide public, and the annual accounts are prepared within a few weeks of the end of each financial year. In addition, the branch manager or cashier of some rural banks in India can give an instantaneous statement of the position of deposits, advances and operating costs of their branch as at the conclusion of the last transaction.

As a bank's product is money, it seems obvious that it should measure its success in terms of money. But enterprise development agencies which deal in training, advice or technology can and should also aim to monitor their day-to-day performance as regularly as a bank or any commercial organisation. In fact, as mentioned already, they should apply and adopt the good business advice which they themselves dispense as part of their training, counselling and extension services to their client groups. This can involve daily evaluation sessions in training courses; regular maintenance of individual client progress records as is recommended for enterprise extension services (Harper, 1984b, p.141), or updating records on training systems such as in the IYB's Monitoring and Evaluation System (ILO, 1994). Such data should be part of the routine duties of field staff's work, and they should also be its primary users. More comprehensive evaluations, such as may be required from time to time by donors, can be carried out using this data as a starting point (Imboden, 1978, p.125), subject perhaps to random checks to ensure its reliability. As a consequence, management should be no more surprised by the results of evaluations than the manager of a well-run company is likely to be surprised by the results of their own annual accounts.

What Measures Should Be Used?

The hypothetical debate between proponents of different methods of evaluation that is presented in an early work on small business extension services (Harper, 1977, p.45) lists most of the indicators which have been referred to in the examples given in earlier chapters. When selecting measures, there is a wide range of possibilities, and the selection will ultimately depend on the specific objectives of the activity and the objectives of the evaluation, as well as on the feasibility of obtaining the necessary information.

Impact indicators are essentially a matter of identifying "proxies" (Boomgard, 1989, p.28) which are regarded as appropriate means of describing and reflecting the effects of an activity, or "measurable indicators" as they are referred to in the logical framework vocabulary. However, the selection of objectives for small enterprise development itself can frequently involve a compromise between measurability and accuracy on the one hand, and the ultimate purpose of the project on the other. It is possible to describe the real purposes of small enterprise development projects and programmes as goals or aims, but it has to be recognised that just as inputs such as loan disbursements or numbers trained are "proxies" for enterprise development, enterprise development is in itself a proxy for the whole complex of welfare, social, economic and political factors that together make up "development". Kilby and Z'mura (1985, p.5) suggest that "the additional income associated with the intermediate index (such as jobs, new businesses or sales) is the true benefit," but even income is not an end in itself. The small enterprises where the income is earned are also a means to an end, just like training or loans.

It is, therefore, important not to abandon measurement because it is difficult, but to try to ensure by the right or optimal choice of players, timing and measures that the evaluation is useful, rather than being so long-delayed that it is only of academic interest (Imboden 1978, p.121), or so imprecise that it is meaningless. This implies that such evaluations are likely to be quite complex. We should remember that many factors that used to be considered impossible to measure, such as gross domestic product, air pollution or the degree of subsidy received by a financial institution, are now considered quantifiable (Feinstein 1994). The problem is not the concept of using targets and indicators themselves, but the use of badly framed or inappropriate targets or indicators.

Critics of quantitative approaches, including USAID (Boomgard, 1989, pp.29–31) and many NGOs, suggest that they tend to overlook and omit social factors such as empowerment or solidarity, and that clients may in fact put a greater value on these intangibles than on increased income as such. It has also been argued (Kilby and Z'mura, 1985) that the focus on measuring the costs of the assistance, as well as the benefits to client enterprises, can divert attention from other more important benefits, such as reduced consumer prices or new services, or from focussing on other costs such as displacement of labour or adverse impacts on other businesses arising from the activities of those which have benefited. In any event, the costs involved in developing and implementing an evaluation system should not be excessive or distract attention away from core project implementation activities.

An SED training evaluation study in South Africa (Wilgespruit Fellowship Centre, 1993) also stresses the danger of using simplistic quantitative measures as a yardstick against which others' performance may be judged. Any form of evaluation must be seen primarily as a tool for the use of those whose work is being evaluated, and qualitative measures — which mean little to uninformed outsiders or donors — may be immensely valuable to those who are actually carrying out the programme itself.

Attempts have been made to quantify the indirect factors resulting from a project's operations, but it can be difficult and costly, and may involve so large a number of assumptions that the whole basis of any conclusions may easily be questioned. It is more practical, if less rigorous, to assume that improvements in the economic performance of small enterprises that operate in highly competitive market-places can be taken as a proxy for improved efficiency which ultimately benefits the economy as a whole. In addition, a person whose business is more successful as a result of a support activity will also thereby be more empowered, or be better able to work towards the social changes which she or he considers important.

The earlier examples have illustrated a wide range of indicators, such as businesses started, client income or the status of family nutrition. It is important to remember that as well as being valid, reliable, relevant, sensitive, specific and timely, indicators must also be cost-effective (UN ACC Task Force, 1984, p.38). In one case, for instance, ACCION decided that any benefits to employees of client enterprises would not be considered, not because they were unimportant but because of the time and expense of obtaining the necessary information (Jayasundere, 1995, p.229).

The cost of some enterprise development projects is a great deal more than the benefits to the clients could ever be, and evaluation itself costs money and time. It is obviously absurd to spend more on evaluating an activity than on the cost of the activity itself (Harper, 1984b, p.169), unless it is a special pilot or prototype case where the possibility of major future replication must be rigorously investigated.

It is also important to distinguish between those measures that can and should be part of a regular management information system, and those which are a necessary part of evaluation but for which data cannot be expected to be collected regularly as part of day-to-day operations.

We have earlier drawn many analogies between the world of small enterprise projects and the world of business itself. Indeed, SED project staff, as well as donors, should "practise what they preach" and use appropriate business tools in managing their own development operations. The business model suggests that as much information as possible should be collected and used as part of the routine of management, and that non-routine items, such as physical stock-checks or external audits, should be minimised. This approach may be appropriate for a profit-seeking business, but where there are wider social objectives (such as empowerment of the disadvantaged) or potential problems (such as client drift or mobility), factors which are not associated with the profitability of the programme may require their own form of regular monitoring that may or may not be consistent with the efficient operations of the project. In some cases attention to such important factors may create a conflict with progress towards long-term economic and commercial sustainability.

Other evaluations of factors such as quality of life may require special one-off studies, to be carried out on a sample basis and often requiring specialist expertise in fields such as nutrition, health or education, which lie outside the discipline of enterprise development. Decisions on these forms of evaluation will of course depend on the objectives of each programme, but it is part of the nature of development projects that they should be evaluated by criteria which go beyond the immediate sustainability of the project itself.

Earlier chapters have described measures used to evaluate entrepreneurship training and technology development programmes, as well as to assess the level of sustainability reached by credit programmes. These are by no means the only forms of enterprise development activity, and it may be useful at this point to consider some measures which are appropriate for other types of programme. These lists are not intended to be exhaustive, but they should serve to illustrate the wide range of indicators that are available. As stated above, the actual choice must depend on the objectives of each programme, the stage that has been reached, and prevailing local circumstances.

In the Annexes at the back of the book we provide some examples of survey instruments which have been used in a number of different locations. The Micro and Small Enterprise (MSE) Registration and Evaluation Form (Annex 1) was produced for the FIT Programme (Wesselink, 1995b). It has the benefit of providing a simple "bird's eye view" of the entrepreneur's situation before and after "the project" (the project could be a training or exchange programme, among other activities). In Annex 2 a more detailed questionnaire is provided in the form of a Summary Sheet of the post-training evaluation of ILO's Start Your Business (SYB) programmes in Zambia and Zimbabwe.

SED Evaluation is as concerned with the impact and sustainability of both implementing and partner organisations, as it is about the enterprises themselves. We have included a sample of an evaluation form for implementing agencies. This was developed by FIT for use with its Micro and Small Enterprise (MSE) groups and partner organisations (Wesselink, 1995a).

Evaluating Other Non-financial Support Programmes

Box 8.1 lists some different types of programmes, as well as their appropriate evaluation indicators. Any comprehensive evaluation of a project should also provide indicators of the cost-benefit relationship and its cost-effectiveness; cost coverage or recovery from earnings, and programme sustainability so as to ensure continuation of the service after the withdrawal of donor assistance. This is relevant unless the objective is a short-term one, such as the resettlement of refugees, or the client group is such that total cost coverage is unlikely ever to be possible, as with small enterprise activities for seriously disabled people.

Whichever indicators are chosen, it still remains to be decided whether and how the evaluation will ensure that the effects have been caused directly as a result of the efforts of the project, and what necessary adjustments need to be made to take account of timing or other factors, and how, if at all, these effects can be related to whatever was spent to achieve them.

Box 8.1: Impact measures for other types of enterprise development programmes

---

Extension Services: (see Harper 1977 and 1984b; Gibb and Manu, 1994)
  Staff recruited and trained
  Enterprise clients visited
  Advice given
  Advice followed
  Clients' willingness to pay
  Clients' wage and profit increases

Incubators and industrial estates: (see Lalkaka and Bishop, 1996)
  Premises secured or built
  Premises occupied
  Business started (and cost per enterprise)
  Jobs created (and cost per job)
  Other services used
  Clients graduated to economic rentals
  Clients graduated to commercial property

Marketing Assistance: (see Craig and Cerone, 1994)
  New markets/customers identified
  Sales volume achieved
  Repeat orders secured
  Catalogue entries finalised
  Marketing costs covered
  Outlets and distribution channels adopted
  Cost-effectiveness of promotional activities

Small Business Association Development: (see Kobb, 1995, 1996)
  Paid-up membership achieved
  Subscription income earned
  New services developed and used
  New services paid for by members
  Rate of member participation

Chapter 9

Guidelines for the Future

Evaluation should only be undertaken if it is useful, and the same principle applies to the suggestions made throughout this book. It is appropriate, therefore, to summarise some of the more important conclusions that can be drawn from the previous chapters. These conclusions are stated in the form of prescriptive guidelines, not because they are viewed as being beyond question, but because this presentation is calculated to provoke thought, including possible disagreement, and to help the reader to come to conclusions which she or he can take ownership of. In this way the book should be used as a basis for practical action.

1. Only carry out evaluations where the process and the results will be of practical value to some or all the parties involved. This is particularly true of the owners, employees and customers of small enterprises.

2. Ensure that the benefits likely to arise from any evaluation are equal to or greater than the costs of doing it, including all aspects of the costs to field staff and clients.

3. Evaluation criteria, and the bases upon which evaluation will be carried out, should be built into the design of the project.

4. Base the evaluation on the original objectives of the activity, but be alert to unexpected results. The relevant objectives include not only the planned benefits to small enterprises, but also whether the activity is intended to be a pilot or a one-off intervention, or to develop a permanent institution along commercially sustainable lines.

5. Select appropriate indicators for each stage of project implementation, and use these to monitor progress as well as to evaluate results and efficiency.

6. Decide which indicators should be routinely collected by programme staff and which will need specialised or one-off measurement.

7. Evaluate continually at the lowest possible level, and ensure that the evaluation system is self-correcting whenever possible.

8. In true marketing fashion, encourage clients to monitor the quality of the services provided, as well as to demand improvements; this can usually be done by ensuring that they make some payment for the service.

9. Involve clients in the choice of indicators, as well as in the provision of data and discussion of results.

10. Check that the intended target group are in fact those who are benefiting from project support.

11. Quantify costs and benefits whenever possible.

12. Ensure that project staff and clients are aware of the full costs involved in providing the development intervention. This encourages responsibility on the part of project staff, as well as generating client pressure for a quality service.

13. Relate benefits to costs in some way, however difficult it may appear, in order to ensure that clients are receiving value for the money that is being spent on their behalf.

14. Make some attempt to isolate the effects of what is being evaluated, possibly through the use of control groups or in some other practicable way.

15. Where appropriate monitor progress towards programme sustainability (e.g., by comparing annual cost recovery rates), but also continue to monitor the progress towards achieving the project's original development objectives.

16. Ensure that the findings of any evaluation exercises are acted upon, otherwise errors and weaknesses are likely to repeat themselves.

Finally, it may seem like a harsh test of efficiency and value for money, but one crude evaluation measure is to divide the total cost of a project, including all overheads, by the total number of clients who have benefited. Then ask, and answer honestly, this question:

"Was this sum of money well spent, or would the clients have benefited more if they had been given the money and allowed to spend it as they wished?"

b

ANNEX 1: The MSE Registration and Evaluation Form

Worksheet 1: MSE Registration and Evaluation Form

Name : _____
Activity : _____
Location : _____

Gender: m/f

A. *Registration* (Before the project)
Date: ____ / ____ / ____

1. Which people work with you in this activity ? Specify:

Gender	Name
m/f	_____
m/f	_____
m/f	_____
m/f	_____

2. Do you and your employees work the whole year long in the business?

	Which months?	Total no. of people working	Days/ month	Hours/ day
High season				
owner:	___	___	___	___
Employees:				
full-time	___	___	___	___
part-time	___	___	___	___

B. *Evaluation* (After the project)
Date: ____ / ____ / ____

1. In the past _____ months, how has your business volume changed?
_____ a lot (more than 50%)
_____ a little (less than 50%)
a. increased _____
b. decreased _____
c. no change _____

2. In the past year, how much did you and your employees work at this acitivity?

	Which months?	Total no. of people working	Days/ month	Hours/ day
High season				
owner:	___	___	___	___
Employees:				
full-time	___	___	___	___
part-time	___	___	___	___

(continued)

ANNEX 1 *(continued)*

Low season
owner: _____
Employees:
full-time _____
part-time _____
Zero activity _____

3. Besides metal-working, what other activities earn you the most money?

Activity	Which months?	Days/months	Hours/day
1. _____	_____	_____	_____
2. _____	_____	_____	_____

4. Wage rates.

a. What wage rate would you pay to an average worker in your business? _____

b. What do farm labourers earn during your high season?
(i) male _____ (ii) female _____

Low season
owner: _____
Employees:
full-time _____
part-time _____
Zero activity _____

3. As a result of the increase (decrease) in your business, did you decrease (increase) other activities? If so,

Activity	Which months?	Days/months	Hours/day
1. _____	_____	_____	_____
2. _____	_____	_____	_____

4. Wage rates.

a. What wage rate would you pay to an average worker in your business? _____

b. What do farm labourers earn during your high season?
(i) male _____ (ii) female _____

5. What assets do you own in this business
   a. land _____
   b. building _____
   c. equipment _____

5. Have you purchased any business assets in the past period? No/Yes
   a. land _____
   b. building _____
   c. equipment _____

6. As result of the project activity, has there been any change in the number of:
   a. new product designs, techniques and technologies acquired and introduced? Specify: _____

   b. new business contacts acquired? Specify: _____

   c. new fit/fpd farm implements and tools/food processing device introduced, produced, and sold? Specify: _____

Worksheet 2: General Data Form

A. *Before project support activity*

1. Inflation rate
   Consumer price index : _____
2. Deposit interest rate : _____
3. Project area general economic activity indicator
   * sales at the local general store
   * amount of bank deposits
   * agricultural output
   * number of arriving taxi passengers per month
   * other : _____
     Kshs : _____

B. *After project support activity*

1. Inflation rate
   Consumer price index : _____
2. Deposit interest rate   : _____
3. Project area general economic activity indicator
   Kshs : _____
4. Costs of project support activity:
   a. direct activity costs : _____
   b. indirect activity costs : _____
   c. total activity costs : _____
   d. beneficiaries : _____
   e. cost per beneficiary : _____

Source: Wesselink (1995b)

ANNEX 2: Summary Sheet of the Post-training Evaluation of ILO's SYB Programmes in Zambia and Zimbabwe

Training Activity Attended

1. **Which SYB training activities did you follow:**

ANSWER	SCORES	TOTAL
TOPE* and Follow-up		
TOPE only		
Part of the above (not fully attend)		
Other		

2. **How could you describe the follow-up services provided to:**

ANSWER	SCORES	TOTAL
Follow-up seminar and individual assistance		
Follow-up seminar only		
Individual assistance only		
Other assistance		

3. **Do you feel you have received enough follow-up assistance from the SYB trainer(s) to finalize your feasibility study?**

ANSWER	SCORES	TOTAL
Definitely enough		
It would have been better if more received		
Definitely *not* enough		

The Business Idea

4. **What was your original business idea?**
5. **What was your business idea after the TOPE?**

ANSWER	SCORES	TOTAL
Remained the same		
Changed after the TOPE		

* Training of Potential Entrepreneurs

6.   If your business idea has changed, can you explain why?

ANSWER	SCORES	TOTAL
Lack of skills		
Money problems		
Market may not be good for the idea		
Personal problems		
Other		

Your Feasibility Study

7.   Have you finalised your feasibility study?

ANSWER	SCORES	TOTAL
Yes		
No		
Partly		

8.   Did you use the ILO SYB Feasibility Study Booklet to develop your feasibility study?

ANSWER	SCORES	TOTAL
Yes		
No		

9.   Did you submit a request for external funding?

ANSWER	SCORES	TOTAL
Yes		
No		

10.   What kind of financing institution did you submit your feasibility study to?

ANSWER	SCORES	TOTAL
NGO		
Commercial Bank		
Government		
Other		

11.   Was your feasibility study approved?

ANSWER	SCORES	TOTAL
Yes, the full amount I requested in the proposal was approved		
Yes, but only part of what I requested was approved		
No, it was rejected		

12.   If your feasibility study was approved, what was the amount approved? (*Please convert to US dollar equivalents*)

ANSWER	SCORES	TOTAL
Below $ 100		
$ 100-500		
$ 500-1,000		
$ 1,000-3,000		
$ 3,000-6,000		
$ 6,000-10,000		
Over $ 10,000		

13.   If your feasibility study was *not* approved, what were the reasons given by the financing institution?

ANSWER	SCORES	TOTAL
Feasibility study was not complete/too low quality		
Not enough collateral		
Too high/low budget		
No reasons given/I do not know		
Other reasons		

14.   If your feasibility study has *not yet* been approved, what are you doing in the meantime?

ANSWER	SCORES	TOTAL
I will start anyway with the money I have		
I will wait till I get the loan		

15. How much owner's equity did you contribute to your business? (*Please convert to US dollar equivalents*)

ANSWER	SCORES	TOTAL
None		
Below $100		
$500–1,000		
$1,000–3,000		
$3,000–6,000		
Over $6,000		

Your Business

16. Have you started your business?

ANSWER	SCORES	TOTAL
Yes		
No		

17. If not, why did you not start?

ANSWER	SCORES	TOTAL
Not enough funds		
Preparations not ready yet		
Changed plans		
Other reasons		

18. What kind of business have you started? or What kind of business were you planning to start?

ANSWER	SCORES	TOTAL
Retail		
Wholesale		
Manufacture		
Service Operation		
Agriculture		
Other		

19.   What legal form of business have you started/were you planning to start?

ANSWER	SCORES	TOTAL
Sole Proprietorship		
Partnership		
Limited Company		
Cooperative		

20.   How many people do you employ *full time and for a salary* in your new business?

ANSWER	SCORES	TOTAL
None		
One paid employee		
Two paid employees		
Three paid employees		
Four paid employees		
Five paid employees		
More than five	Write down the numbers given	

21.   How many people do you employ *part time and for a salary* in your new business?

ANSWER	SCORES	TOTAL
None		
One paid employee		
Two paid employees		
Three paid employees		
Four paid employees		
Five paid employees		
More than five	Write down the numbers given	.

22.   Do you employ any people outside your family?

ANSWER	SCORES	TOTAL
No		
Yes: One		
Yes: Two		
Yes: 3-5		
Yes: 6-10		
Yes: 11-15		
Yes: More than 15		

Feasibility Study Quality Assessment

23.   Could the potential entrepreneur make the feasibility study available for you to look into?

ANSWER	SCORES	TOTAL
Yes		
No		

24.   Does the feasibility study contain all the information?

ANSWER	SCORES	TOTAL
Yes, all sections are complete		
No, a little is missing *(1-4 sections incomplete)*		
No, a lot is missing *(more than 4 sections incomplete)*		

25.   What are reasons given for not completing of the sections in the feasibility study?

ANSWER	SCORES	TOTAL
Has not had time to finish		
Does not know how to complete it		
Does not see a need to fill it out		
Does not have a particular reason		
Other reason(s)		

26.   Is the feasibility study easy to understand and clear to the reader?

ANSWER	SCORES	TOTAL
Very clear		
Could be improved		
Is difficult to follow		

Source: ILO SYB (1997)

ANNEX 3: MSE Group/FIT Partner Evaluation Form

Date:_____/_____/_____

I. Particulars of MSE group/Partner organisation

Name of MSE group/FIT Partner: _____

Location: _____

Main activities: _____

How many (staff) members does the group/organisation have:

Female:_____ Male:_____

II. Evaluation question for MSE group/Partner organization

- How many of each type of activity have been held?

#	FIT activity
	Exchange visits; brokering workshops; enterprise linkages
	Shows
	Rapid Market Appraisal
	Subsector Analysis
	Communication with farmers
	Training
	Research
	Other, specify:

- How many participants did attend the activities?

Participants	# female	# male
End-users		
Entrepreneurs		
Group/partner staff members		
Others, specify		
Total:		

- What is the number of products (produced by metalworkers supported by FIT) which have been tested or displayed by your group/organisation? Please specify:

_____

_____

- Was the collaboration successful between FIT and your group/organization for each of the activities? Why (not)?

- How has the activity strengthened your group/organisation?

	new memberships
	trained staff members, specify in which activities:
	spin-off effects resulting in new activities
	improved group cohesion
	improved participation of group members in collective planning and problem-solving
	increased awareness of sustainability: fees for services
	contribution to innovation and/or leveraged interventions
	contribution to the implementation of a number of policy recommendations
	others, specify:

- What is the contribution of your group/organisation in the costs of the activity (staff time/salaries, administrative costs, etc.)?

- What are the the direct income benefits of the activity for your group/organisation (e.g. from new memberships)?

- Is your group/organisation willing to cover (a percentage of) the costs of future activities? About what percentage?

- What are lessons to be drawn? How can the activity be improved?

- What are the plans of your group/organisation to replicate, change, expand or develop based on this specific activity in the next two years? (and, what are the implications for income and staffing?)

Specific activity-related questions

- In the case of a subsector analysis (SSA): are SSAs implemented?; What is the role of SSA in your group/organisation?

- In the case of new technologies/designs introduced: What is the number of different designs available, and number of designs copied and used by your group/organisation?

#	
	different designs available
	designs copied and used

Source: Wesslink, (1995a)

Bibliography

Aaker, J and   Shumaker, J (1994), *Looking Back and Looking Forward, A Participatory Approach to Evaluation*, Heifer Project International, Little Rock.

ACCION/Calmeadow (1988), *An Operational Guide for Micro-enterprise Projects*, ACCION/Calmeadow, Toronto.

Acharya, BT (1990), *Rural Industrialisation, A Catalyst for Action*, Himalaya Publishing House, Bombay.

Angelsen, A and Sumaila, UR (1995), *Hard Methods for Soft Policies, Environmental and Social Cost-benefit Analysis*, Chr. Michelsen Institute, Bergen.

Awasthi, D and Sebastian, J (1992), *Evaluation of Entrepreneurship Development Programmes*, EDI-I, Ahmedabad.

Awasthi, D and Sebastian, J (1996), *Evaluation of Entrepreneurship Development Programmes*, Sage Publications, New Delhi.

Bandaranayake, K, Amarapale, PG and   Herath, GB (1996), Evaluation Report on CEFE programmes conducted by SLBDC in Ratnapura IRPD, SLBDC, Colombo.

Bolnick, B and Nelson, E (1990), Evaluating the Economic Impact of a Special Credit Programme in Indonesia, KIK/KMPK in Indonesia. *Journal of Development Studies*, June 1990.

Boomgard, J (1989), Taking Stock of USAID's M-E Stocktaking Portfolio, Background and Conceptual Overview, AID Evaluation Special Study 66, USAID Washington.

Brown, R (1995), The Graduate Enterprise Programme; Attempts to Measure the Effectiveness of Small Business Training. *British Journal of Education and Work*, VIII, 1, 1995.

Buzzard, S and Edgcomb, E (1987), *Monitoring and Evaluating Small Business Projects*, PACT, Washington.

CARE (1995), Introduction to the SEAD Evaluation Framework, Annex F to Proposal for Expansion of Women's Economic Development Project, CARE Kenya, Nairobi.

Chowdhury, MM and Abed, FH (1991), Credit for the Rural Poor, the case of BRAC in Bangladesh. *Small Enterprise Development*, Volume 2, number 3, 1991.

Chua, Ronald T and Llanto, Gilberto M (1996), *Assessing the Efficiency and Outreach of Micro-finance Schemes*, ILO Geneva.

Craig, K and Cerone, F (1994), *An Evaluation of the PRIDE/FIT Brokering Workshop for MSEs*, ILO/TOOL, Amsterdam/Geneva.

Cushion, N (1995), Measuring the Success of Small Business Training, paper presented at 18th ISBA National Conference, Paisley, Scotland.

Devarajan, S (1995), *Project Appraisal at the World Bank*, World Bank, Washington.

Economic Planning Associates (1992), *Triennial Review of Intermediate Technology Development Group*, London.

Eigen, J (1992), Assistance to Women's Businesses, Evaluating the Options. *Small Enterprise Development*, Vol. 3, no. 4, 1992.

European Union Evaluation Unit (1993), *Manual on Project Cycle Management*, EEC, Brussels.

Famiyeh, JA (1995), *On-going Project Evaluation with the Logical Framework*. University of Science and Technology, Kumasi, Ghana.

FAS (undated), Community Employment Open Learning Unit on "Evaluation", (1993), Final report of the joint evaluation mission of the self-employment programme for training institute and the local enterprise development agency programme. (Indonesia), ACIL, Hawthorn (Australia).

Feinstein, ON (1994), 'To measure or not to measure', paper presented at World Bank Conference on Evaluation and Development, Washington.

Ferrera, MD (1994), Report of the Evaluation Mission, Small Enterprise and Informal Sector Promotion, CMB/92.010, Phnom Penh.

Feuerstein, M-T (1986), *Partners in Evaluation*, MacMillan, London.

Forss, K and Bjern, L (1994), *Evaluation of the Improve your Business Programme*, Swedecorp, Stockholm.

Freeman, HE (1979), *Evaluating Social Projects in Developing Countries*, OECD, Paris.

Gibb, Allan A (1991), *Defining Success in Entrepreneurship Development Programmes: A Guide to a Model Approach*, ILO Geneva.

Gibb, Allan A and Manu, George (1994), The Design of Extension and Related Support Services for Small-scale Enterprise Development in International Small Business. Journal Vol. 8 number 3, 1994.

Goldmark, S and Rosengard, J (1987), *A Manual to Evaluate Small-Scale Enterprise Programmes*, USAID, Washington.

Gray, M (1995), *The Evaluation of Technical Assistance for Development in Eastern and Central Europe*, Civil Service College, Ascot.

Haggblade, S (1992), A Proposal for Monitoring Small Enterprise Promotion, *Small Enterprise Development*, Vol. 3, no. 4, 1992.

Harper, A (1995), Community Banks, the Management of Village On-lending Groups in Northern Pakistan, paper presented at Finance against Poverty Conference, Reading 1995.

Harper, M (1974), The Development of a Cost-effective Extension Service for Small Businesses: A Kenyan Experiment, unpublished Ph.D. thesis, Nairobi.

Harper, M (1977), *Consultancy for Small Business*, IT Publications, London.

Harper, M (1984a), *Entrepreneurship for the Poor*. I.T. Publications, London.

Harper, M (1984b), *Small Business in the Third World*, Wiley, Chichester.

Harper, M (1996), Nineteen years of Enterprise Development Training, in *CEFE Magazine*, Frankfurt, October 1996.

Harper, M and Mahajan, V (1992), Assessment of Entrepreneurship Development Programmes in India, report submitted to Overseas Development Administration, London.

Harper, M and Mahajan, V (1995), 'Evaluating Entrepreneurship Development Programmes in Practice', *British Journal of Education and Work*, VIII, 1, 1995.

Hileman, M (1994), *An Evaluation of the PRIDE/FIT Exchange visit Programme*, ILO/TOOL, Amsterdam/Geneva.

Hulme, D (1995), Finance for the Poor, Poorer or Poorest, Financial. Innovation, Poverty and Vulnerability, paper presented at Finance against Poverty Conference, Reading.

ILO (undated) Guidelines, Part Two: Evaluating a Project. Undated mimeo, ILO Geneva.

ILO (1986), Assistance to Employers' Organisations. Internal Evaluation Report, Geneva.

ILO (1987a), *Improve Your Business, Evaluation Report on Impact in Kenya*, IYB/ILO Nairobi.

ILO (1987b), *Committee on Operational Programmes, Assessment of Selected ILO Projects Concerning Rural Small Industrial Enterprises*, ILO Geneva.

ILO (1988), *Higher Productivity and a Safer Place to Work —* Workbook and Manual, Geneva.

ILO (1989), Formation des cadres de banque au financement des PME en Afrique de l'Ouest, external evaluation. ILO Geneva.

ILO (1990), Income Generating Activities for Refugees in Eastern and Central Sudan, Revolving Loan Scheme, Evaluation Report, ILO Geneva.

ILO (1992a), *ENT/MAN Survey: Networking for Entrepreneurship Development*, ILO Geneva.

ILO (1992b), *Republic of Ghana, IYCB*, Evaluation Report, ILO Geneva.

ILO (1994), *IYB Monitoring and Evaluation Kit*, ILO Harare.

ILO (1995a), *Promoting Employment*, Report of the Director General, ILO Geneva.

ILO (1995b), *Gender Issues in Micro-enterprise Development*, ILO Geneva.

ILO (1995c), *Design, Monitoring and Evaluation of technical Cooperation Programmes and Projects: A Training Manual*, Geneva.

ILO (1996a), The "Improve Your Business" Programme Worldwide: Achievements and Experiences (draft paper prepared by P. Samuelsen), Geneva.

ILO (1996b), Design, monitoring and evaluation of technical cooperation programmes and projects — A training manual, Geneva.

ILO SYB Project (1997), *Evaluation of Start Your Business (SYB) Programme in Zambia and Zimbabwe*, Harare, Zimbabawe.

Imboden, N (1978), A Management Approach to Project Appraisal and Evaluation. OECD Paris.

IYB (1995), Bulletin Nos. 22-3, January-March and April-June 1995, Harare.

Jayasundere, R (1995), *Savings and Credit 3, Monitoring and Evaluation*, IRED, Colombo.

Kilby, P and Z'mura (1985), Searching for Benefits, AID Evaluation Special Study 28, USAID Washington.

Kobb, D (1996), Impact of GTZ/SIDO's Crafts and Small Enterprise Promotion Program on Income, a Follow-up Study, Tanga.

Kobb, D (1995), Impact of GTZ/SIDO's Crafts and Small Enterprise Promotion Program on Income, Tanga.

Kolshorn, R (1994), The CEFE Evaluation, Brainstorm, *CEFE Newsletter*, GTZ, Eschborn, January 1994.

Lalkaka, R and Bishop, J (1996), *Business Incubators in Economic Development*, UNDP, New York.

Levitzky, J (1986), *World Bank Lending to Small Enterprises, A Review*. World Bank, Washington.

Livingstone, I and Tribe, M (1995), The Discount Rate and The Economic Appraisal of Projects with Long Time Horizons. Paper presented at DPPC Bradford.

Marsden, D and Oakley, P (eds.) (1990), Evaluating Social Development Projects, Oxfam, Development Guidelines no. 5, Oxford.

Mburugu, Julius B.M. and Thiongo, John M. (1996), Promotion of Entrepreneurship and Self Employment in Kenya, paper presented at ILO Workshop on Lessons from Small and Medium Sized Enterprises (SME) Development, Nairobi, Kenya.

McBer and Company and Management Systems International (1984), Entrepreneurship and Small Enterprise Development, First Annual Report, Washington.

· McClelland, D and Winter, D (1971), *Motivating Economic Achievement*, Free Press, New York.

McNamara, R (1968), *On Gaps and Bridges, in The Essence of Security, Reflections in Office*, London, Hodder and Stoughton.

Moran, D (1995), Valuing Environmental Change, The Contingent Valuation Method and Project Planning. Paper presented at DPPC Bradford.

Mosley, P (1993), *Metamorphosis from NGO to Commercial Bank, The Case of Bancosol in Bolivia*, Working Paper No.4, Department of Economics, University of Reading.

Mwaniki, B (1995), *Evaluation of Jua Kali Agricultural tools programme*, ILO, FIT Geneva.

Neshamba, F (1995), Transitions in the Informal Sector, unpublished research paper, Cranfield School of Management.

Otero, M (1989a), *Microenterprise Assistance Programmes: Their Benefits, Costs and Sustainability,* ACCION, Washington.

Otero, M (1989b), *A Question of Impact: Solidarity Group Programmes and Their Approach to Evaluation*, ACCION, ASEPADE/PACT, Tegucigalpa.

Padaki, Vijay (ed.) (1995), *Development Intervention and Programme Evaluation: Concepts and Cases*, Sage Publications, New Delhi.

Price, C (1995), Discounting and Project Appraisal; From the Bizarre to the Ridiculous, paper presented at Conference on Development Projects, Issues for the 1990s, Bradford.

Reichert, Chr. and Herath, GB (1996a), Organising and Marketing CEFE Training in Sri Lanka — prospects for sustainability, paper prepared for Cape Town International CEFE Symposium and Conference.

Reichert, Chr. and Herath GB (1996b), Some Ideas on a Research and Development-oriented CEFE M&E system, paper presented at Cape Town CEFE conference, Colombo.

Rhyne, E (1994), A New View of Finance Programme Evaluation, in Otero M and Rhyne E (eds.), *The New World of Micro-enterprise Finance*, Kumarion Press, West Hartford.

Romanovsky, J. et al. (1985), *Review of the Pilot Project for SED for Refugees in Lesotho.*, ILO Geneva.

Rubin, F (1995), *A Basic Guide to Evaluation for Development Workers*, Oxfam, Oxford.

Samson, Marcia R (1996), Monitoring Development Impact for Improved Project Design, in *ADB Review* of Sep.-Oct. 1996, Manila.

Schumacher, EE (1973), *Small is Beautiful*, Blond and Briggs, London.

SEFCO (1996), A Case Study in Small Scale Enterprise Support Services, a paper presented at the ILO Workshop on Lessons from Small and Medium Size Enterprise (SME) Development, Nairobi, Kenya.

Sell, A (1992), Planning and Evaluation of Projects in Countries with High Inflation Rates, Project Appraisal, Vol. 7, no. 1.

SENA (Servicio Nacional de Aprendizaje) (undated), *A Business Improvement Programme for Small and Medium Enterprises*, Bogota, Colombia.

Stern, N (1994), The World Bank as Intellectual Actor, typescript 1993, quoted in George S, and Sabelli F, *Faith and Credit*, Penguin.

Storey, D (1987), The Role of Government in Promoting SMEs, paper presented at European Small Business Seminar, Genoa.

Sweeting, P, et al. (1993). Final report of a joint evaluation mission of the self-employment programme for training institutions and the local development agency programme (Indonesia), ACL, Hawthorne (Australia).

Taimni, KK (1994), Meeting Small Enterprise Training Needs, *Small Enterprise Development*, Vol. 5, No. 2.

Tanburn, JP (1995), *Pointers to Success: A Framework for Evaluating the Impact of the FIT Programme*, ILO/TOOL, Amsterdam/Geneva.

Tomecko, J and Kolshorn, R (1996), Promoting Entrepreneurship — the CEFE method, *Small Enterprise Development Journal*, Vol. 7, No. 4, December 1996.

UN ACC (1984), Task Force on Rural Development, Panel on Monitoring and Evaluation, Guiding Principles for the Design and Use of Monitoring and Evaluation in Rural Development Projects and Programmes, Rome.

UNDP/ILO Interman Project (undated), Guidelines for Preparing Case Studies on Effective Entrepreneurship Development Programmes/Approaches, ILO Geneva.

USAID (1995), Assessing the Impacts of Microenterprise Interventions: A Framework for Analysis, working paper no. 7.

Webster, L (1990), Fifteen Years of World Bank Lending for Small and Medium Enterprises, in *Small Enterprise Development*, Vol. 1, no. 1.

Wesselink, B (1995a), *Guidelines for Evaluating FIT Activities Including Evaluation Forms*, ILO/TOOL, Amsterdam/Geneva.

Wesselink, B (1995b), *Quantifying Impact of MSE Support Services at the Enterprise Level*, ILO/TOOL, Amsterdam/Geneva.

Westborg Consult (1996), *Evaluation of Diaconia-FRIF and its Programme for Employment Creation through Small Enterprise Promotion and Employment Exchance*, La Paz, Bolivia, Oslo.

Westhead, Paul and Storey, David (1996), Management Training and Small Firm Performance: Why is the Link So Weak, *International Small Business Journal*, Vol 14. No. 4, issue No 56, Jul-Sep 1996.

Wilgespruit Fellowship Centre (1993), *Business Counsellor Training Evaluation, January 1993*, Roodepoort.

Wilmshurst, J (1995), An ODA Perspective on the Past and Future of Project Appraisal, paper presented at conference on Development Projects, Issues for the 1990s, Bradford.

World Bank Operations Evaluation Department (1990), *The Aga Khan Rural Support Program in Pakistan*, World Bank, Washington DC.

Yaron, J (1992), *Development Finance Institutions, A Public Interest Analysis*, World Bank, Washington.

Index

www.ingramcontent.com/pod-product-compliance
Lightning Source LLC
Chambersburg PA
CBHW070936030426
42336CB00014BA/2694